TheShepherd purpose books series

Foreword By Dr Sam Abah

Purpose of Success

Everyone has what
it takes to succeed

TheShepherd
LOHO-U-TER SHADRACH

Purpose of Success
...Everyone has what it takes to succeed

Published by:
Scrollhouse Publishing Firm.
A Service of TheShepherd Loho-u-Ter Resources
Zaria Road, Mission Street
Farin Gada, Jos.
Plateau State

ISBN: 978-978-54440-3-2

For special discounts for bulk purchases, please contact:
08053468634 | 08032988168
Scrollhouseng@gmail.com
Visit www.scrollhouse.com.ng for eBooks

Layout and Cover Design: TheShepherd Loho-u-Ter Shadrach

Printed Nigeria by Triune Concept

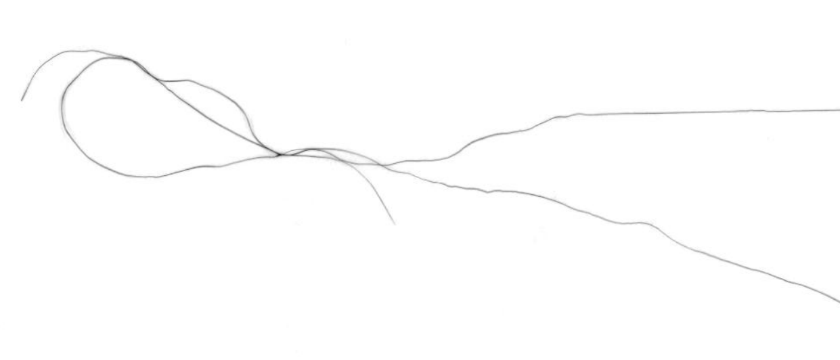

Dedication

To my mentors:
Michael O. and Princess Monivi Amamieye.
Your encouragement has made me take positive
steps to be who I was born to be

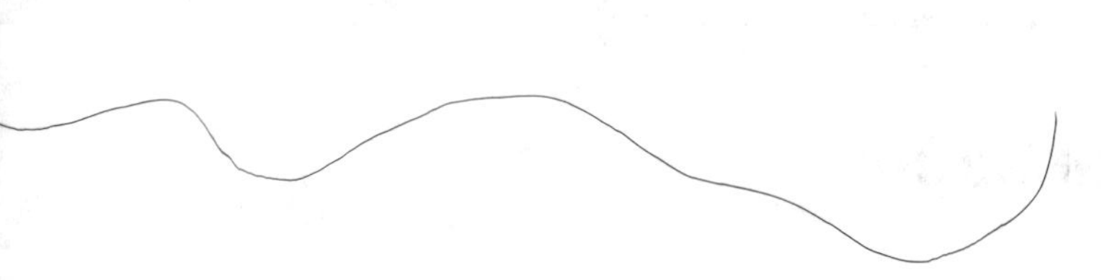

Acknowledgments

I give thanks to the giver and preserver of life, who has given me tremendous strength to use hours of study and the staying power on the computer to be able to write this book. You have connected me to the right material and human resources to make this book possible.

I appreciate my family for believing in me. Your love and understanding have encouraged me to give attention to making sure that this book was written.

I acknowledge people who have sat under my teachings and are practically applying my principles of success in their lives in one way or the other.

There are authors and characters I cannot bypass anytime the discourse of success comes up. Your writings and endeavours have been of encouragement to me and have influenced this book, and I want to say thanks.

My thanks go to the team of editors: Lydia Torkwase Chile, Iliya Mangvwat, and Muyamba Mathias and the team at Scrollhouse who have made sure that this work came out as at when due, with the quality I desired.

My appreciation goes to Michael O. and Monivi Amamieye. Your encouragement has made me take positive steps to be who I was born to be by putting together the organization I have established as a major platform for my teachings.

My special thanks finally go to my readers. I appreciate the confidence you have in me, and in my ability to influence your life in the area of success.

Foreword

What is the "winning edge"? Do you have the "winning edge"? No, it's not fair hitting you straight away with this kind of question. Welcome the "Purpose of Success "by my friend, TheShepherd Loho u-Ter Shadrach, one of Nigeria's upcoming authors. The author says, "Don't underestimate yourself. You are more powerful than you can imagine!" Yes, I found this at the tail end of this beautiful and rich book—*Purpose of Success*. However, to me, it is about the greatest thing said by the entire book by this dynamic young African writer, Shadrach.

The world, particularly, the Black race, Africa, Nigeria, your State, my village; we are guilty of this grave crime! When you underestimate yourself you never put out your best because, in the first place, you cannot imagine yourself being better than where you are and what you have! It is a prison, an open prison!

My God! the entire world loses so much. Families lose, Companies, Schools, Teams, NGOs, Governments, Clubs, everybody loses a lot when they minimize themselves.

Why do people minimize themselves? Why are we so determined in underrating our capabilities? Why are we more comfortable with failure, or underachievement than sustained success?

Why is it easier to find people who will help you to give up or postpone your dreams than people who will assist you to pursue your dreams through thick and thin? Ignorance! Yes, ignorance is still a gigantic rampaging enemy, in spite of massive information flowing across the globe. One particular type of ignorance that is most deadly, is the ignorance of the routes to sustainable enjoyable transferable success. The book, "Purpose of Success" is timely because it is designed to kill that giant of limitation in your life!

The author has done a marvellous job of killing ignorance around SUCCESS. Beautiful stories, succinct quotes, crystal clear illustrations, numerous authorities on success, these and more spices make the reading sweet as you journey through this resource. The book is so well organized and subtitled that you can decide to study any of the sections or start from the end backward, and still be richly informed and inspired.

I enjoyed the Four "C's", and you will not forget them easily. It encapsulates the entire message of the book. It is the kernel of the author's Breakthrough Strategy: "Creativity, Commitment, and Consistency bring about a Consummation of all efforts".

When you finish reading the book, you do not need to meet the author: a deliberate, focused young man driven by a crystal clear purpose, to empower men and women in such a way that their lives glorify God.

Success matters to all of us—young and old, men and women, sure-footed or unsure of our chances. For people who desire to honour God, knowing the most efficient and effective route to good success is even more needful. Welcome to this beautiful garden with so many attractive ripe fruits. I enjoyed every minute of this book. Please enjoy your journey into THE PURPOSE OF SUCCESS.

Dr. Sam Abah
Team Leader, Grassroot Africa.

Content

1. Introduction

However difficult life may
seem, there is always something
you can do and succeed at.
-Stephen Hawking

I SAW YOUR SUCCESS LIFE ACTIVATED THE moment you held this book in your hand and decide to start reading. For some reason, out of all the books on success; you decided that this is the one you would read. Somehow, you knew that you will find useful information here to make you succeed. You decided to increase your knowledge, therefore, your energy to succeed is stirred up.

knowledge is cumulative

It is said, *'Knowledge is power,'* that is why the most successful people in the world are constantly increasing their knowledge in the areas of their profession. A source says that knowledge is cumulative. This, therefore, means that a person who wants to be more successful will gather more knowledge. Tracy says regarding the accumulation of knowledge that:

> Once it exists, it does not cease to exist. It becomes available to more and more people and it grows exponentially. Every new piece of knowledge reveals connections and interconnections with other areas of knowledge in a self-reinforcing and accelerating pattern. Each breakthrough in knowledge creates new opportunities that expand and multiply as that knowledge is exploited.[1]

Reading this book will lead you to exploit one of the greatest resources on success you will ever read. It is a compendium of knowledge about success from different people who have succeeded in their lives and the laws that guided them to reach their pinnacle of success. If you also want to succeed in your field of endeavour, you will then need to do what other

---

[1] Brian Tracy. *The 100 absolutely Unbreakable laws of business success,* (San Francisco: Berrett-Koehler Publishers, Inc., 2000), 1.

successful people do, to get the results successful people get.[2]

Be determined to win

To get to your desired goals of success, you must determine to be a winner. Never think of losing or think like losers. The loser sees only problems in his or her project that will make him/her fail. The winner sees the storms as situations to glide unto success. He or she is obsessed with the concept of winning and dares to do things differently that gives him or her the winning edge. This concept says, "Small differences in ability can lead to enormous differences in result."[3] The 'winning edge' concept is what stands a person out between being successful or mediocre.

This book, *'Purpose of Success'* will not only tell you the purpose of success, but will give you the laws that successful people have used to succeed in life, in a very simple way, that applying them will not be cumbersome.

---

[2] Tracy. *The 100 absolutely Unbreakable laws of business success,* xii.
[3] Tracy. *The 100 absolutely Unbreakable laws of business success,* 2.

The moment you started reading this book, you have started taking advantage of its content to place you on the pedestal of success which people around you will want to identify with. Envision yourself a winner, because everything about your life is about to change. You are about to leap to a level of success that will only be limited to how far you have envisioned you are going to get.

Success is possible

Success is possible! and it is predictable! When I see your antecedents and measure them with your current status in conjunction with what you think and say, relating such with the materials you read, the things you listen to, and the programs you watch, I can confidently say you are a success even if you are down there at the bottom of the pyramid.

To be successful in life is a choice that can only be made by you. I really do want you to come out of mediocrity—if you are still there; to a place of great wealth that is measured beyond money and this life: The wealth that generations will tap into and such wealth will follow you to the great beyond because you would have known the purpose of success.

This book is loaded with many of the most powerful ways to make you succeed, and the greatest of all is that you will get the real purpose why you need to succeed and what you should use your wealth for. The misunderstanding of the purpose of success has made people live wasteful lives in the name of success without really knowing what success really means.

Do not let anyone tell you otherwise

Friend, your toil, your desire, and your aspiration to succeed are about to burst out. Never look down on where you are right now. Never let anyone tell you that you will not succeed in your endeavours. Never let yourself dictate for you based on your condition. Poverty is a mentality and so is success. Your ability to succeed is based on your ability to think, believe, and act towards your thoughts of success. Come with me, there are things you need to know!

2. Success: What is it?

Success consists of going from failure
to failure without loss of enthusiasm.
-Winston Churchill

SUCCESS MEANS DIFFERENT THINGS TO different people. All the different definitions of success cannot all be right, especially if they are not defined in line with what the Creator sees success to mean. The subscribers of "The Dreamer's Guide" Motivation newsletter were asked to define success and all of them gave their different perspectives of what success meant to them. These are some of their responses:[4]

---

[4] These responses are from:
Motivation for Dreamers, "What is Success," [cited August 18, 2015] Online: www.motivation-for-dreamers.com/whatissuccess.html.

Divergent definitions

Isaac Alex Phiri's definition of success is as follows:

i. Reach to a place where your dreams were pointing
ii. When you get what you really wanted
iii. When you triumph over your adversaries, obstacles, and barriers of life.

Geoffrey Nkhoma defines success to be, "the attainment of real joy or happiness. This joy comes about when we see that the people we love (God and family) are happy".

To Janett Kalale, True success is truly measured by what you have left when you go to the grave. For the living, the quest to succeed is an ongoing process for nothing in human life is ever perfectly complete until nothing more can be done. This is because to me success means achieving the best results possible to my utmost satisfaction having exploited my potential in whatever area of my consideration and therefore being able to move to a new area for nothing more can be done in the old.

Simon Abwino defined success as being able to obtain what you require or want to do at a specified time. It also means the ability to meet your needs at a specified time.

Humphrey says: to many people, success is measured in terms of monetary wealth. That is achieving financial independence and prosperity. But he feels that success should encompass the following areas:

i.   Happiness in family life and in marriage for the married people
ii. Having a healthy relationship with God almighty and confidence of eternal life
iii. Happiness or satisfaction in the occupation or vocation one may have.
iv. Rich in respect from one's friends and other relationships such as from workmates or workers as the case may be.

What comes to mind

For many people, when they hear of success, this is what comes to their mind according to John C. Maxwell:

i.   The wealth of Bill Gates,

ii.   The physique of Arnold Schwarzenegger (or Cindy Crawford)
iii. The intelligence of Albert Einstein,
iv.   The athletic ability of Michael Jordan
v.   The business prowess of Donald Trump,
vi.   The social grace and poise of Jackie Kennedy
vii. The imagination of Walt Disney
viii. The heart of Mother Teresa[5]

In line with what Maxwell says is the definition of peoples understanding of success, the business dictionary defines success to be:

Achievement of an action within a specified period of time or within a specified parameter. Success can also mean completing an objective or reaching a goal. Success can be expanded to encompass an entire project or be restricted to a single component of a project or task. It can be achieved within the workplace, or in an individual's personal life.[6]

---

[5] John C. Maxwell. *Your road map for success,* (Nashville: Thomas Nelson, inc, 2002), 5-6.
[6] Business Dictionary, "Definition of Success," [cited August 18, 2015] Online: www.businessdictionary.com/definition/success.html,

Good but not enough

All the above-mentioned definitions of success have one or many good things to tap from. The challenge is, many definitions of success have little or nothing to say about a person's purpose for living. If you do not really know what you were created for, how then can you be said to have succeeded? What have you succeeded in doing? You may as well succeed in doing another person's job.

To truly succeed means you need to find your purpose for living and live out the life you were designed to live. The success I refer to here is beyond financial wealth, a special feeling, material possessions, power, or achievements. These are not the true pictures of success. The misunderstanding of the true picture of success has pushed people to dedicate their whole lives to pursuing money and fame.

People who narrow success to financial wealth never get enough. The industrialist John D. Rockefeller was a man who gave out more than $350 million in his lifetime. This great industrialist was asked how much money it will take to satisfy him and he said,

"Just a little bit more."[7] The richest king who ever lived had said, *"Whoever loves money never has money enough; whoever loves wealth is never satisfied with his income..."*[8]

Real definition of success

So, if money, power, achievements, and possessions are not true success, what then is success? Since I came about Maxell's definition of success, it has given answers to the question of success more than any answer I ever got. It fits into what the creator would define success based on the totality of the life manual.

Maxwell defines success as, "knowing your purpose in life, growing to reach your maximum potential, and sowing seeds that benefit others."[9] Without understanding your purpose of living, maximizing your potential and sowing seeds of kindness, your money, affluence, political power, material abundance, and all your achievements put together is a big loss. I must say that such a life of affluence

---

[7] Maxwell. *Your road map for success*, 6.
[8] Ecclesiastes 5:10. New International Version.
[9] Maxwell. *Your road map for success*, 11.

without knowing the purpose of success is actually a misappropriation of life.

Ask yourself

It is, therefore, needful to know your purpose for living. Ask yourself what you do in life that gives you joy and still makes you glorify your maker, maintaining a vertical relationship with him and a horizontal relationship to humanity, yet your joy is not depleted as you serve him, serve humanity and take care of the ecology. If you will answer this question properly and honestly, that could be your purpose for living. You could find further details as you do the diagnostic test on how to discover your purpose in my book, *"Purpose of Living."*

When you discover your purpose for living, you will need to develop your potential as much as you can to help you define your purpose. Everyone has great potentials locked inside of him or her. Your ability to harness them to achieve your purpose puts you on advantage as against people who allow their potentials to lie fallow. Developing your potential may take time and it is a gradual process. But with the help of the one who put them there, you will reach your zenith.

He put them there

Your potentials are specially woven into you by your creator. The wealthy Job, afraid for his life at a point of distress, confirmed the creative ability of the almighty as he cried out saying:

> Don't you remember how beautifully you worked my clay? Will you reduce me now to a mud pie? Oh, that marvel of conception as you stirred together semen and ovum —what a miracle of skin and bone, muscle and brain! You gave me life itself, and incredible love. You watched and guarded every breath I took.[10]

This great man recognized that everything about his being is in God. The blueprint of your life is known to your maker because he created you. The almighty says of you, *"The people I made especially for myself, a people custom-made to praise me."*[11] In a very pictorial manner, Myles Munroe says:

> Your life is like a cup of drink served to the world by our great creator. The drink is the awesome, untapped, valuable, destiny-filled treasure, gifts,

---

[10] Job 10:9-12. The Message.
[11] Isaiah 43:21. The Message.

and talents of potential buried within you. Every minute, day, month, and year is an interval of opportunity provided by God for the pouring out of another portion of yourself until you have exposed all his precious treasure that makes you unique[12]

Friend, you are custom-made! You are the only you, and you have great potentials that if properly harnessed, there is no telling how successful you will become in life. If you must, therefore, be successful in this life and in the hereafter, connecting with the creator who knows and formed you is the only guarantee for permanent and real success.

What are potentials

Now, what are potentials by the way? The word comes from the word potent which means strong, powerful, effective, and forceful. God is called Omnipotent. The Omni in the Omnipotent means 'always'. So, God is always strong, powerful, effective, and forceful. He has within him the potential for all that is, had been, or ever will be.[13] If

---

[12] Myles Munroe. *Maximizing your potentials*, (Nassau: Destiny image publishing, 2002), 28.
[13] Myles Munroe. *Understanding your potentials*, (Nassau: Destiny image publishing, 2002), 31.

your maker is always potent—strong, powerful, effective, and forceful. The energy to succeed, therefore, is hinged on connecting with him and your attitude about living a successful life. Munroe describes attitudes as:

> The mind-set or mental conditioning that determines our interpretation of and response to our environments." It's our way of thinking. It is also important to understand that attitude is a natural product of the integration of our self-worth, self-concepts, self-esteem, and sense of value or significance. In essence, your attitude is the manifestation of who you think you are. [14]

Think like a king or queen

Who do you think you are really? Who you think you are will make you who you think you are. I have gone to places where underdevelopment is so thick, but have seen people who think like kings and queens. I once met a man who was paralyzed, deaf and dumb but his attitude was that of a great man.

---

[14] Myles Munroe. *The spirit of leadership: cultivating the attitudes that influence human action* (New Kensington: Whitaker house, 2005), 51.

Does the name Nick Vujicic ring a bell? I love this man. He has the attitude of a successful person. Nick was born on 4 December 1982 with tetra-amelia syndrome, a rare disorder characterized by the absence of all four limbs. Nick struggled mentally and emotionally as well as physically as a growing child, but eventually came to terms with his disability and, at the age of seventeen, started his own non-profit organization, *"Life without Limbs."* Vujicic presents motivational speeches worldwide that focus on life with a disability, hope and finding meaning in life. He also speaks about his belief that God can use any willing heart to do his work and that God is big enough to overcome any disability.[15]

Discover and succeed

Vujicic has discovered his purpose in life and is making sure that his untapped potentials are used to fulfill his purpose for living. Vujicic may not be super rich financially, but for the fact that he knows his purpose, he is making sure that his potentials are expressed, and is involved with sowing seeds of kindness in the lives of people, you could say Vujicic is a successful man.

---

[15] Wikipedia, "The life of Nick Vujicic," [cited August 18, 2015] Online: http://en.wikipedia.org/wiki/Nick_Vujicic

Before we will go into how you can succeed, let me remind you that success is way beyond money, material wealth, power, and influence. It is understanding your purpose, maximizing your potentials, and sowing seeds of kindness which will be a deposit into your celestial bank. This wealth shall speak for you when you finally go for it at the time of withdrawal.

3. Succeeding: Tripartite Laws of Success

Success depends upon previous
preparation, and without such
preparation, there is sure to be failure.
-Confucius

A LAWLESS SOCIETY IS A CHAOTIC society. Can you imagine a society without the military without police, without leaders or laws? That society will swallow its inhabitants. That is why from the beginning of time, the creator had set laws in motion that automatically yield their results when we act in relation to them.

You do not need to tell an object to come down when you throw it up. The law of gravity in the everyday common sense means, "The force which causes objects to fall onto the ground." The way I would talk about gravity in a non-professional way is that, everything that goes up must come down.

Clearing the confusion

Success also has laws and many such laws are written down. These laws are written by successful people who have tried out certain things and have succeeded. There are so many of these laws that one gets confused about how to abide by them.

Looking at the various laws of success that are written by those in business, life coaching, leadership, money-making, marketing, management, ministry, and all kinds of endeavours, I have come to the conclusion that there are actually only three laws to succeed in anything you do. The bulk of the other laws of success that are propounded by various successful people are just a further explanation of the three. The three laws are what I call the *'Tripartite Laws of Success'*. You can apply them in any field of life and they will work just fine. These laws are:

i. Creativity,
ii. Commitment, and
iii. Consistency.

There is a fourth part of these laws which is the result of abiding by the three laws. I call the fourth part **'Consummation.'**

These laws of success are from the principle of the 4 C's— Loho-u-Ter breakthrough strategy. The first three C's of the Loho-u-Ter breakthrough strategy are what I am referring to here as the tripartite laws of success. This principle is put together in a sentence in this way:

Creativity, commitment, and consistency bring about a consummation of all efforts.

Live by them

I have lived by these principles. Many successful people also live by them, and if you are succeeding in some way, you are also living by them. You may not necessarily coin them the way I have, they may have different names and a different twist but however you call your laws of success, it all boils down to creativity, commitment, and consistency which consummates in success.

In the next three chapters, I will address the tripartite laws of success in more detail as compared to what I have written in the other purpose books. It gives me joy that someone is ready to succeed; and that person would be you. I will, therefore, need you to give in some time and more attention from this point. Shut out every distraction that may cut you off from these timely truths that will make you succeed forever.

4. Law one: Creativity

Victory has a thousand fathers,
but defeat is an orphan.
-John F. Kennedy

DEFEAT STARTS FROM THE MIND. THE manifestation of what is seen outwardly starts on the inside. My first law of success attacks defeats on the inside. This law says:

I believe that creativity is of God. Therefore, anyone with creative ideas; who seeks to achieve excellence can attain anything in life to the maximum no matter the obstacles.

This law has its roots from a life manual quote that says, "*...it's God's Spirit in a person, the breath of the Almighty One that makes wise human insight* *possible."*[16] The life manual further says as related to the creation of humans that *"God formed Man out of dirt from the ground and blew into his nostrils the breath of life. The Man came alive — a living soul!"*[17] Wow! What a gift. Can you imagine how loaded you are?

The Creator spoke

Look at it this way: The beautiful things around you were created by God as he uttered the word of his mouth—speech. Look at how he created the world by speech and his ingenuity as recorded in the opening chapter of the life manual.

- God spoke: "Light!" And light appeared.... Day One.

- God spoke: "Sky! In the middle of the waters; separate water from water!"... Day Two.

- God spoke: "Separate! Water-beneath-Heaven, gather into one place; Land, appear!"

---

[16] Job 32:8. The Message.
[17] Genesis 2:7. The Message.

- God spoke: "Earth, green up! Grow all varieties of seed-bearing plants, every sort of fruit-bearing tree." And there it was... Day Three.

- God spoke: "Lights! Come out! Shine in Heaven's sky! Separate Day from Night. Mark seasons and days and years, Lights in Heaven's sky to give light to Earth." And there it was... Day Four.

- God spoke: "Swarm, Ocean, with fish and all sea life! Birds, fly through the sky over Earth!"... Day Five.

- God spoke: "Earth, generate life! Every sort and kind: cattle and reptiles and wild animals — all kinds." And there it was:

- God spoke: "Let us make human beings in our image, make them reflecting our nature... God created human beings; he created them godlike, Reflecting God's nature. He created them male and female. God blessed them: "Prosper! Reproduce! Fill Earth! Take charge! ... God looked over everything he had made; it was so good, so very good! ... Day Six.[18]

You were formed to create

Remember we had established that *"...it's God's Spirit in a person, the breath of the Almighty One that makes wise human insight possible."*[19] And that, *"God formed Man out of dirt from the ground and blew into his nostrils the breath of life. The Man came alive — a living soul!"*[20] In other words, you can imagine things and see to it that they come out as thought by your creativity and actions.

Your maker's breath in you gave you your soul—will, mind, and emotions. Your creative ability is therefore from him. Those who assumes they are not creative are like saying, they are empty. As long as you have the breath of life, you are creative. All that you need to do is to discover and put to practice the potentials that are there in you. To properly understand and be more creative, there is a need to understand what creativity is all about.

---

[18] For details of the creation story, read genesis chapter 1 and 2. The selected quotes are from The Message Bible.
[19] Job 32:8. The Message.
[20] Genesis 2:7. The Message.

Creativity defined

California State University Northridge has sampled various definitions of creativity as follows:[21]

Robert E. Franken defines creativity as the tendency to generate or recognize ideas, alternatives, or possibilities that may be useful in solving problems, communicating with others, and entertaining ourselves and others.

Robert W. Weisberg says, "creative" refers to novel products of value, as in "The aeroplane was a creative invention." "Creative" also refers to the person who produces the work, as in, Picasso was

---

[21] The various definitions of creativity are provided by the California State University Northridge from these books and authors:

i. *Human Motivation*, 3rd ed., by Robert E. Franken: (page 396)
ii. *Creativity - Beyond the Myth of Genius*, by Robert W. Weisberg. (page 4)
iii. *Creativity - Flow and the Psychology of Discovery and Invention* by Mihaly Csikszentmihalyi. (Pages 8, 25-26).

For further details, Visit:
California State University Northridge, "Definition of Creativity," [cited August 19, 2015] Online:
http://www.csun.edu/~vcpsy00h/creativity/define.htm.

creative." "Creativity," then refers both to the capacity to produce such works, as in "How can we foster our employees' creativity?" and to the activity of generating such products, as in "Creativity requires hard work."

Weisberg further says "All who study creativity agree that for something to be creative, it is not enough for it to be novel: it must have value or be appropriate to the cognitive demands of the situation."

Mihaly Csikszentmihalyi rather gave ways that "creativity" is commonly used before giving a definition and says:

i. Persons who express unusual thoughts, who are interesting and stimulating - in short, people who appear to unusually bright.

ii. People who experience the world in novel and original ways. These are (personally creative) individuals whose perceptions are fresh, whose judgments are insightful, who may make important discoveries that only they know about.

iii. Individuals who have changed our culture in some important way. Because their achievement is by definition public, it is easier to write about them. (e.g., Leonardo, Edison, Picasso, Einstein, etc.)

After Csikszentmihalyi gave ways of how "creativity" is commonly used he further gives his definition of creativity as follows. "Creativity is any act, idea, or product that changes an existing domain, or that transforms an existing domain into a new one...What counts is whether the novelty he or she produces is accepted for inclusion in the domain."

It boils down to thoughts

If these definitions confuse you, give creativity your meaning. I will simply say creativity is having a great idea. It is looking inwards to bring out something wonderful that people can identify with. Everything about creativity boils down to thoughts. A creative person is a thinker.

I will try to identify with several authors and quotes on various laws of success that I still consider being creative. Each of the words we will be discussing is in one way or the other connected to thinking, and that is how you know these words are still talking about creativity.

Various strands of creativity

a.   Creativity is desire

If you really want to be successful, you must desire to be successful. Arina Nikitina says, *"If you want something badly enough you will get it."*[22] Every desire starts with a thought, it starts with imagination. Everyone who wants to be successful must begin to desire to be. Please do not forget that success is not limited to money but working in accordance with your purpose, maximizing your potentials, and sowing seeds of kindness in the lives of people.

I am sure you know the meaning of desire but just to juggle your mind I will re-iterate it again. The Oxford Dictionary online defines desire as a strong feeling of wanting to have something or wishing for something to happen.[23] When you really desire, you will work

---

[22] Arina Nikitina. *The five laws of success*, (United Kingdom: White Dove Books, 2006), 3.
[23] Oxford Dictionary, "Definition of Desire," [cited August 18, 2015] Online:
www.oxforddictionaries.com/definition/english/desire.

toward actualizing your desire. Success starts at the point of desires. Desire makes you create mental pictures, deepen your faith, and make you look towards the mighty creator.

The life manual confirms this position saying:

> ...what things soever you desire, when you pray, believe that you receive them, and you shall have them.[24]

> O Lord, You have heard the desire and the longing of the humble and oppressed; you will prepare and strengthen and direct their hearts, You will cause Your ear to hear.[25]

> God can do anything; you know — far more than you could ever imagine or guess or request in your wildest dreams! He does it not by pushing us around but by working within us, his Spirit deeply and gently within us.[26]

This last quote says our maker grants us our desire and imaginations *"not by pushing us around but by working within us, his Spirit deeply and gently within us."* God works on you from what

---

24 Mark 11:24. King James Version.
25 Psalms 10:17. Amplified Bible.
26 Ephesians 3:20. The Message.

you are made of. He works with the deposit of what is deep within us.

Some people have carried desire to the extreme where the creator is not involved. The heat of their desire is so much that they can kill for what they desire. Their quest for success has made their various arenas war zones. The life manual says of such people that:

> You desire and do not have; so you kill. And you covet and cannot obtain; so you fight and wage war. You do not have, because you do not ask. You ask and do not receive, because you ask wrongly, to spend it on your passions.[27]

The desire that is outside of God's design for your life can be injurious. But the proper heat of a person's desire is what moves such a person from a mediocre to a successful person. If your desire is pointed in the right direction, there is nothing stopping you from reaching your success goals. I agree with Nikitina on this point that "Desire overcomes obstacles to success. Desire makes molehills out of mountains. No matter what stands in the way, it is moveable."[28]

---

[27] James 4:2-3. Revised Standard Version.
[28] Nikitina. *The five laws of success*, 4.

b.   Creativity is responsibility

Right from the beginning of time, people are obsessed with blame games. They hardly own up for a wrong or a failure in their lives. They will always look for someone to blame. May I tell you that "you are completely responsible for everything you are, for everything you'll become and everything you achieve,"[29] says Tracy. Folding your hands and blaming everybody and everything for your misfortune is not the way out of failure. The way out is to take responsibility for everything.

Now, let me be more practical. Do you know that you become what you think most of the time? Your mind has the ability to be selective in what it processes. The person responsible for that control is not even God but you. Whatever you see, hear, feel, smell and taste have the ability to affect your thought pattern either positively or negatively. People can force you to do many things against your will but no one has the ability to force you to think. That is why you are absolutely responsible for your thoughts.

---

[29] Tracy. *The 100 absolutely Unbreakable laws of business success*, 37.

A creative person takes responsibility for his or her actions. I have noticed that people who criticize and blame people for the failures in their lives hardly progress. Rather than thinking creatively, their minds are clouded with hate towards other people and situations around them whom they assume is the reason for their failures.

In many cases, people are careful with such people who refuse to take responsibility for their actions. When a person continues to refuse responsibility, such a person makes more enemies as the blame game continues. If you must achieve your success goals, you must be willing to take responsibility for the things you do and the things you refuse to do.[30]

Responsibility is also a state of the mind. Since no one forces you on what you should think about, you cannot blame anyone for being where you are. If you must, therefore, succeed, you will need to creatively think on how to accept higher levels of responsibility. The higher you aspire to be, the greater the responsibility.

---

[30] Tracy. *The 100 absolutely Unbreakable laws of business success,* 38.

c.   **Creativity is clarity**

When I was not very clear about my purpose for living, I kept moving from one job to the other, trying one thing or the other to see what was more appropriate for me at any given time. Friends and family kept suggesting to me what to do. I had worked with two different architectural firms before I had a diploma in Fine and Applied Arts. I tried to travel to Ghana to work for an organization but things did not work out. I and my family moved to Jos Plateau state to work in a sales company but did not feel it was the right thing for me to do. Prior to this, I unofficially volunteered to work for Peace House, Fellowship of Christian Students, and Calvary ministries –CAPRO.

I was moving from place to place and changing work because I did not know exactly what to do. At a point, I had an art studio, a printing outfit and also provided telecommunication services to the public. I can go on and on. All these were trial and error. My experiences helped me to a point I know exactly which direction in life I have to turn to. I now understood the law of clarity and my life has taken shape.

Clarity is actually "The quality of being certain or definite."[31] The ability to understand where you are going and have your destination's mental picture is what is called clarity. That is also creative. When you are clear about your direction in life; when you are clear about why you are on earth. You let go of all other things you had done before to concentrate on your purpose. When the tent maker understood and was clear about his purpose in life, he made sure that all distractions were laid aside. And he gave this caution:

> You know that in a race all the runners run, but only one runner gets the prize. So run like that. Run to win! All who compete in the games use strict training. They do this so that they can win a prize—one that doesn't last. But our prize is one that will last forever. So I run like someone who has a goal. I fight like a boxer who is hitting something, not just the air. It is my own body I fight to make it do what I want. I do this so that I won't miss getting the prize myself after telling others about it. [32]

---

[31] Oxford Dictionary, "Definition of clarity," [cited August 18, 2015] Online:
www.oxforddictionaries.com/definition/english/clarity.
[32] 1 Corinthians 9:24-27. Easy to Read Version.

Paul—the tent maker clearly said: *"he runs like someone who has a goal."* When you do not seem to have a goal, you are aimless. You are like a boxer who just aims at nothing. When you aim at nothing, that is exactly what you will get—NOTHING.

What do you really want to achieve? What are your goals? There is a simple way of becoming more specific about your goals:

Step one: Discover and decide exactly what you want to achieve in the different areas of your life. Be exact and specific.

Step two: Write down in detail what you have discovered and decided.

Step three: Set specific deadlines for what you want to achieve. If it is a large goal, break it down into sub-deadlines and write them down in order.

Step four: Make a list of everything you can think that will aid you and you have to do to achieve your goal. Add new items to the list as you continue to think about them.

Step five: Prioritize the items on your list, placing them in the proper sequence.

Step six: Take action immediately on the most important thing you can do in your plan. **This is very important.**

Step seven: Do something every day that moves you towards the attainment of one or more of your important goals. Maintain the momentum.[33]

When I got this concept from Brian Tracy, I made up my mind that I was going to write a minimum of two hundred books in my lifetime. My sub-deadline was a minimum of five books in a year. I took another step and posted my goal on Facebook and Twitter. Luckily for me, a friend challenged me and called me names. He told the whole world that I was showing off. How it was not possible to write five books in one year. I was not happy the way he went on and on about it, and I quickly remembered what my pastor told us of how his uncle used to call him a dull chap, but that triggered and awoke his potentials. As of today, Bala Jidanke has a Ph.D.

------

[33] Tracy. *The 100 absolutely Unbreakable laws of business success,* 271-272.

What this friend who challenged my goals on Facebook did not know was that since that day, I make sure I do not write less than twenty pages of the books I am working on in a week. This is also a book in the series of books I am writing on "purpose." The other ones in the series so far are (i) purpose of living, (ii) purpose of insight, (iii) purpose of money, (iv) purpose of suffering, (v) purpose of fitness, (vi) Purpose of Leadership and (vii) Purpose of Entrepreneurship. Other books in the series will keep coming as I get inspired. It is now very clear to me what I should do in my writing profession.

Do you want to be creative? Then be clear on what you want, be specific, and do not allow room for distractions along the way to divert you from your main catch.

d.   Creativity is positive beliefs

I had worked in a particular geographical location where many people there have a strange way of responding to greetings. When you greet them good morning, or good afternoon, or good evening and you ask them how they are doing. Their response is usually something like this. *"Is only suffering"* or *"nothing has added."* Implying that nothing has added to the suffering you already know they are going through. Their belief system is weird. Many of the people in this location believe that their life is meant to be miserable.

Do you see yourself to be in the group of people I have mentioned above? What you see is what you will get. Your belief system actually makes you who you are. If you believe you are unsuccessful you will be unsuccessful. If you believe you are successful, that is who you will be.

Belief is actually "Something one accepts as true or real; a firmly held opinion."[34] Your opinion about life, marriage, education, wealth, and everything around you shapes your life towards the direction of your beliefs. Your environment, gender, nationality, work, or events are inconsequential. Anthony Robbins says the meaning we attach to those events is what counts. Those meanings will shape who we are today and who we will become tomorrow.[35]

---

[34] Oxford Dictionary, "Definition of belief," [cited August 18, 2015] Online:
www.oxforddictionaries.com/definition/english/
[35] Anthony Robbins. *Awaken the giant within,* (New York: Free Press, 1991), 74.

Robbins further says. "Beliefs are what make the difference between a lifetime of joyous contribution and one of misery and devastation. Beliefs are what cause some individuals to become heroes, while others "lead lives of quiet desperation."[36]

A person who channels his or her life towards turning the negativity in every ugly situation around is creative. I consider every event in my life as a trigger to achieving my goals no matter how ugly the situation. This predisposition has given me the ability to trust God gifting's in me, to do anything my heart is set on doing that will give glory to my maker.

Tracy concurs with my predisposition saying, "You always act in a manner that is consistent with your beliefs, especially your belief about yourself."[37] He further says,

> Your beliefs act like a set of filters that screen out information that is inconsistent with them. You do not necessarily believe what you see, but rather you see what you already believe. You reject information that

---

[36] Robbins. *Awaken the giant within*, 74.
[37] Tracy. *The 100 absolutely unbreakable law of business success*, 17.

contradicts what you have decided to believe.[38]

Belief is not denial but "something one accepts as true or real; a firmly held opinion."[39] Your opinion of success will be what will give you the needed edge to succeed.

e.   Creativity is preparation

Preparation is very key to achieving your goals of a successful life. Preparation also starts from the mind. When a person's mind is not prepared for success, trickles of success will make such a person wild. Especially if it involves financial success. Many of the people who accidentally got money by way of inheritance or other means ended up being poor because they did not know how to go about preserving and making more money; because of their lack of preparation.

To prepare is to get ready. A creative person will prepare his or her mind for success. Sometimes

---

[38] Tracy. *The 100Absoluetely unbreakable law of business success*, 17.
[39] Oxford Dictionary, "Definition of belief," (cited 18 August, 2015).

preparation will require you to make some changes in your mind or even physically. For a person who intends to start a business, such a person may begin to read about the particular business and get to know other folks who are also involved with the same business for clarity. This preparation gives a person the opportunity to minimize failures. When the proper questions are asked regarding the particular venture you intend to get involved with, you will avoid many of the failures of the people who had trodden the path you are intending to tread.

Shabby preparation will produce shabby results, which is why you must get the relevant information in the area of your goals to help you prepare properly. If you want to write a book, for instance, you will need to know the purpose for which you want to write the book. You will prepare an outline for your book. If you are going to be using a computer, you will need to buy one or at least borrow. If you are in a developing nation that has the challenge of power supply, you will need an alternative source of power supply.

Other aspects of the preparation will involve reading other books that discusses the topic which you intend to write about so that you will have an idea of what other people are saying as it relates to your topic. This will be the initial preparation. Subsequent preparation will be with publishers you will want to use, the quality of the book, how to market the book and such kinds of things.

Preparation is a key component in the creative process. You must not assume that things will go on well and jump into pursuing your goals. Prepare as much as it depends on you no matter how small the goal you want to achieve may seem to be.

f.   Creativity is making decisions

The moment you decided to think positively about your destiny, the day you got tired of living a mediocre life and decided to come out of the life of losers was the day you started succeeding. The challenge many people have that keeps them perpetually as failures is the ability to decide. They find themselves in a terrible mess, but the will to decide to come out is just not there.

A creative person will think of life in a more positive light and decide to aspire for his or her goals. The indecisive person asks too many *What if* questions. Such a person will ask, what if I don't succeed. What if I don't get money for this project? What if people don't give me attention? What if I start and don't have the capacity to finish? Too many 'what ifs", so many doubts. The life manual says,

> ...Anyone who doubts is like a wave in the sea, blown up and down by the wind. Such doubters are thinking two different things at the same time, and they cannot decide about anything they do. They should not think they will receive anything from the Lord.[40]

Your ability to be obsessed with living the life you were created to live and deciding you will do something about it no matter how small, is the spark that makes you think of the great ideas I call creativity.

g. Creativity is purpose

The purpose of whatever you are doing is the driving force in doing well in your endeavours. A business without purpose will crash, a marriage without purpose is just a bitter experience, life without purpose is catastrophic. For anything to stand the test of time, the purpose for which you are doing what you are doing should be clearly defined.

---

[40] James 1:6-7. New Century Version.

People sometimes want to know why I am writing. Some have even asked me if this is my main profession. I will tell you what I often say: My main purpose in life is to lead people to a life of holistic abundance. Teaching people to attain this life is very key and books are also some of the resources I use to accomplish my goal. So I write because it is part of the way I will achieve my purpose.

Do you get involved with doing a thing because everybody is doing it? Or do you define the purpose for which you are doing what you are doing? If you want to begin a new experience of success in your career, business, or ministry, start defining the purpose of whatever thing you are doing. But to properly define your purpose, you will need to start with your vision. Troy Waugh says:

A good personal or firm plan must begin with a vision of what you want...in some distant time. A vision is a reality in the future—this is different than a dream... The vision you have established is your "What." Once you can visualize your "What," then develop your "Why." Why do you want to grow to a certain size? Is it to provide you a better life? Provide better service to more clients? Create a firm that can be passed on to another generation of professionals? If you have a strong "Why," you can accomplish almost any "What."[41]

The "what" Waugh is referring to here is your purpose. Creativity all starts with the mind. Unless you see it you won't get it.

h.   Creativity is quality

Most people who know the advantage of quality will identify with something that is of quality no matter how expensive it is. People who fail to understand the advantage of quality end up spending more and denting their integrity.

When I was younger, I went to buy a pair of shoes that were almost five times more expensive than the shoes my contemporaries were wearing at that time. My friend criticized me for being extravagant, and he bought two pairs of shoes. Two of these shoes were not up to half the amount I bought my pair. His shoes looked good but they were not quality shoes.

---

[41] Troy Waugh, *101 Marketing Strategies for Accounting, Law, Consulting, and Professional Services Firms,* (Hoboken: John Wiley & Sons, Inc., 2004), 7.

Shortly afterward, all his shoes spoilt but mine was still strong till the day I gave them out.

When you have great ideas you want to execute, make sure that quality is at the back of your mind. Always remember that quality is better than quantity when you are referring to creativity. People associate you with the quality of things you do, the quality of life you live, and the quality of ideas you associate with. They will in many cases judge you by first impression or what and who you surround your life with.

It is commonly said, "There is no second chance for a first impression." When you think you do not have money to do quality things or you carelessly start working on an idea that does not make sense, by the time you have more money to do the quality things and are more prudent with your ideas, people will judge you based on your antecedences. As you think creatively towards the achievement of your goal, quality must be your watchword. You need to hear this secret from the leaders.

Jack Welch, the long-time Chairman, and CEO of General Electric, has been hailed as the greatest business leader of our era. This great man was obsessed with quality. Robert Slater affirms that "Welch gradually became convinced that being as good as the next guy, or even a little better, wasn't good enough."[42] He quoted Welch to have said:

> We want to be more than that. We want to change the competitive landscape by being not just better than our competitors but by taking quality to a whole new level. We want to make our quality so special, so valuable to our customers, so important to their success, that our products become their only real value choice.[43]

People will associate you with the quality of things you do. It is unfortunate that I associate some names with bad quality. Their quality of speech, their quality of life, and the quality of their products and services. Make sure that your life is lived in such a way that when people talk about you, quality is associated with it.

i.   Creativity is innovations

Marc Chason of Motorola Labs says, "Innovation is creating new value and/or capturing value in a new

---

42 Robert Slater. *29 Leadership Secrets from Jack Welch,* (New York: The McGraw-Hill Companies, Inc, 2003), 98.
43 Slater. *29 Leadership Secrets from Jack Welch,* 98.

way. Value is the keyword, stressing the difference between innovation and invention."[44] Innovations are not inventions really but a new way of repackaging your values.

Innovations here relates to creativity because it is not all the time that you will completely have new ideas. Some of the ideas that you may be working on are someone's, but the twist and the values you create around them would give your idea a facelift.

When telecommunications came to Nigeria, the first companies that were operating told customers that it would not be possible to charge them on per-second billing. You were, therefore, charged per minute even if you used just three seconds to call. A time came when another company was given the permit to operate. From the first day of their launch, they introduced per-second billing. Their innovation brought them a lot of markets, forcing the other company to also adjust to per-second billing. This

---

[44] Innovation management, "How do you define innovation and make it practical and saleable to senior management," [cited August 18, 2015] Online: http://www.innovationmanagement.se/imtool-articles/how-do-you-define-innovation-and-make-it-practical-and-saleable-to-senior-management/

is pure innovation. This company did not invent telecoms but their innovation gave them the needed market.

j.   Creativity is specialization

There are people who are a jack of all trades but master of none. They have tried their hands on every new thing in town. They have tried so many new things that you can hardly identify them with anything. The last time you met them, they were doing one network marketing, the next time you will meet them they will be politicians, and at another instance they are preachers. You can hardly pin them down to anything specific.

When you specialize in a thing, over time you become a master in the same. The first time I had the opportunity to stand in front of people to teach, my knuckles vibrated as I stood there wondering what to do. But years of teaching have taken away my stage fright and I definitely know that I am doing better than I did and with time, I will be better than what I am now.

When you want to go far in life, you will need to think of what you want to invest your time doing. The greatest investment in this life is to spend your life doing what your maker intended you to do. Discovering your purpose will actually help you to specialize in doing what will lead you to your destiny as all your potentials are harnessed towards the specialization of the talent you require to adequately fulfill your destiny.

k.   Creativity is foresight

When a person cultivates the ability to analyze currents situations, assumes what is likely to happen in the future, and take steps to avert possible loopholes for a desired future, the person has foresight.

Many people will assume that foresight is a mere prophecy. The way the word is, it looks like having a foresight. So it is easy to think of foresight as a future that is fixed. On the contrary, foresight invites us to consider the future as something that we can create or shape, rather than as something already decided. *45

---

* This explanation is not necessarily talking about predestination in the discourse of religion.
45 Forlearn, "Foresight," [cited August 18, 2015] Online: http://forlearn.jrc.ec.europa.eu/guide/1_why-foresight/characteristics.htm.

The European Commission gives some characteristics that make foresight distinct from other kinds of future studies as follows:

Foresight is:

Action-oriented: Foresight is not only about analyzing or contemplating future developments but supporting actors to actively shape the future.

Open to alternative futures: Foresight assumes that the future is not pre-determined. The future can, therefore, evolve in different directions, which can be shaped to some extent by the actions of various players and the decisions taken today.

Multidisciplinary: Foresight provides an approach that captures realities in their totality with all the variables influencing them, regardless of the type (quantitative and qualitative).[46]

---

[46] Forlearn, "Foresight," (cited 18 August, 2015).

A creative person will not be idle in participating in the future. Such a person will look at events as they unfold and will think the future, debate the future, and shape his or her future. [47]

I.   Creativity is planning

Danladi Musa defines planning as "the process of putting in order and into decisions now what an organization or group believes they can do in the future. It is a series of decisions taken now for future actions of an organization, a group or an individual."[48]   Planning follows a process and it might take time. The outline of the planning process may follow this pattern that Musa has suggested.[49]

a.   Gather the relevant information about your project and assess your needs.

---

[47] Forlearn, "Foresight," (cited 18 August, 2015).
[48] Danladi Musa. *The strategic Planning Process,* (Jos: CAPRO Media,1999), 11.
[49] The idea of the outline of the planning process is from Danladi Musa. I have however used most of my language and interjected other people's ideas as you will see in the various end notes.

Danladi Musa. *The strategic Planning Process,* (Jos: CAPRO Media, 1999), 38-63.

b.   Clarify your values. "Values are the beliefs that an organization or an individual upholds high and worthy principle as basis for existence. Values speak to the spirit or ethos or ethics of the organization"[50]

c.   Establish your vision. What do you see? What do you want to accomplish? What is the time frame? These questions are very important in establishing the vision for your project, be it a ministry, your life, or a specific project you are pursuing.

An example of a vision will be something like this. Vision of TEAM-Tripartite

"To see people live to their full potentials"

d.   Determine your mission. Your mission is your purpose. Why are you doing what you are doing? Your mission is anchored on your vision. The answer to these key questions will help you determine your mission be it as an organization or an individual.[51]

---

[50] Musa. *The strategic Planning Process*, 41.
[51] My book, *Purpose of living can* help you determine your individual purpose and the purpose for which people are created.

i.   Why do I (we) exist?
ii. What is my (our) service?
iii. Whom do I (we) serve?
iv. What difference will it make if I (we) did not exist?

An example of a mission will be something like this. The mission of TEAM-Tripartite.

"To lead people to a life of holistic abundance"

e.   When you determine your mission, you will set your goals. Again, Musa defines a goal as "a timeless value statement that impresses the desired state where the need or problem no longer exists." I will talk more about goals when I am discussing *'creativity is goal setting.'*

f.   A SWOT analysis follows after goal setting in a planning process. SWOT Analysis helps you understand your Strengths and Weaknesses, and identifies both your Opportunities and the Threats you face. This tool was originated by Albert S. Humphrey in the 1960s. SWOT Analysis can be used in politics, business, ministry, and on your person. SWOT is an acronym for:

S -Strengths

W - Weaknesses

O - Opportunities

T - Threats

Strengths and weaknesses are often internal to you or your organization, while opportunities and threats generally relate to external factors.[52]

One of the reasons why many people do not succeed in life is because they do not fully put their potentials to use. The few who are succeeding are very mindful of putting their potentials to use. But with all the potential everyone has, we also have our weaknesses. If a person knows his or her weaknesses and manages them so that they do not matter in the work they do, they will have fewer problems. And this is what the SWOT Analysis helps a person to accomplish.

---

[52] Mindtools, "NewTMC," [cited August 19, 2015] Online: http://www.mindtools.com/pages/article/newTMC_05.htm.

A source has given possible questions to help you perform a personal SWOT analysis as stated below.[53] Please take a sheet of paper write down answers to the following questions:

Strengths

i. What advantages do you have that others do not have (for example, skills, certifications, education, or connections)?
ii. What do you do better than anyone else?
iii. What personal resources can you access?
iv. What do other people (and your boss, in particular) see as your strengths?
v. Which of your achievements are you most proud of?
vi. What values do you believe in that others fail to exhibit?
vii. Are you part of a network that no one else is involved in? If so, what connections do you have with influential people?

---

[53] This SWOT Analysis is as presented by mindtools.com. I have however modified it slightly to fit my context. To get the unmodified version, visit mindtools.com
Mindtools, "NewTMC," (cited 18 August, 2015).

Be specific and objective in writing down your strengths. Do not just try to write down good stuff about yourself, make sure they are truly your strengths.

Weaknesses

i.   What tasks do you usually avoid because you do not feel confident doing them?
ii. What will the people around you see as your weaknesses?
iii. Are you completely confident in your education and skills training? If not, where are you weakest?
iv. What are your negative work habits (for example, are you often late, are you disorganized, do you have a short temper, or are you poor at handling stress)?
v.   Do you have personality traits that hold you back in your field? For instance, if you have to conduct meetings on a regular basis, a fear of public speaking would be a major weakness.

Hiding your weaknesses will thwart your success goals. Be realistic – it is best to face any unpleasant truths as soon as possible.

Opportunities

i. What new technology can help you? Or can you get help from others or from people via the internet?

ii. Is your industry growing? If so, how can you take advantage of the current market?

iii. Do you have a network of strategic contacts to help you, or offer good advice?

iv. What trends (management or otherwise) do you see in your workplace or your area of endeavour, and how can you take advantage of them?

v. Are any of your competitors failing to do something important? If so, can you take advantage of their mistakes?

vi. Is there a need in your ministry, workplace, company, industry or your field that no one is filling?

vii. Do people complain about something in your workplace or your life? If so, could you create an opportunity by offering a solution?

You might also, look at your strengths, and ask yourself whether these open up any opportunities – and look at your weaknesses, and ask yourself whether you could open up opportunities by eliminating those weaknesses.

Threats

i. What obstacles do you currently face at work or in what you do?
ii. Are any of your colleagues competing with you for projects or roles?
iii. Is your job (or the demand for the things you do) changing?
iv. Does changing technology threaten your position?
v. Could any of your weaknesses lead to threats?

g. After SWOT analysis, it will be appropriate to choose or formulate a strategy for each of the goals you have set. What methods are you thinking of and which resources can you use to achieve your goal? Everyone or an organization that wants to succeed will formulate a course of action for its goals.

h. The next step is to formulate your objectives. You need objectives to achieve your goals. Musa says an objective should be set for each goal in relation to the strategy selected, the resources available and the constraint faced by the individual or organization.

These objectives must be specific with these three key elements:

    i. Time frame
    ii. Target
    iii. Change desired

The objectives should also be SMART.

S – Specific
M – Measurable
A – Attainable
R – Result-oriented, and
T – Time-bound

i.   Identify what you want to do, and thereafter review who you want to bring on board to help in the management. After this is done, you will develop an action plan—how you want to go about to achieve your goal.

j.   It is very important however to develop a budget. When you do not sit down to plan and develop a budget for whatever project you are doing, you could get stuck. The son of man asked a key question in relation to planning and budgeting and he says:

Is there anyone here who, planning to build a new house, doesn't first sit down and figure the cost so you'll know if you can complete it? If you only get the foundation laid and then run out of money, you're going to look pretty foolish. Everyone passing by will poke fun at you: 'He started something he couldn't finish.'[54]

k.   There is a statement attributed to Muhamadu Buhari that he said, "The problem of corruption in Nigeria is lack of supervision."[55] Unfortunately, this statement does not in any way reflect in his life. However, monitoring and evaluation are very key to a planning process. Many people and organizations fail because they do not sit down to ask questions as relating to what they have done with their lives and where to make amends. I believe Donald Trump is financially worthy because he monitors his business and all that he does. I am of this opinion because I saw a caption on a picture in his book *"TRUMP How to Get Rich"* and it says, "Here I am on top of Trump

---

54 Luke 14:28-30. The Message.
55 Paraphrased by the author. I did not hear or read about this statement myself and I do not know how he exactly said it. I am just making sense of it as it is commonly claimed he had said.

World Tower at the United Nations Plaza. I like to check up on things, even without my helicopter."[56]

Evaluation relates to the assessment of an individual or an organization in relation to its goals and objectives over a period of time while monitoring looks at the differences between the planned and the actual.

Creativity is planning and everyone or organizations who do not plan to fail will plan to succeed strategically. Even though most people will not go through the pains to write down their plans, the few who do are at advantage and are more likely to achieve their goals. Planning is not a choice for any person who is aspiring to reach his or her success goals.

m.   Creativity is setting goals

Many people thought I was bluffing when I said I was going to marry Salome in 1998 because campus relationships rarely came to fruition. We had great fellowship as lovers on campus to the envy of many. I knew that destiny brought us together and the

---

[56] Donald Trump with Meredith McIver. *TRUMP How to Get Rich,* (New York: Random House, 2004), 102.

relationship had to step up to the next level. I did not also want to marry disrespectfully by eloping; as was the manner of boys of my age at the time. I was done with my national Diploma in 1998 and was determined to marry in the same year. I set my goal for a wedding the same year for the 21st of November, and all my plans then were to make sure my dreams came through.

You can always hit your target when you aim at something. Aiming at nothing gets you nothing. A person or organization that has no goals is on its decline and final doom, but a person or organization that sets goals gets out of decline, takes control of every situation, is successful, and knows exactly where he or she is coming from and going.

Your goals are better achieved when they go in line with your personal values. As a person, I want to see people reach their full potentials and my responsibility is to lead them to a life of holistic abundance. But I have yearly goals, monthly goals, and daily goals. Sometimes I write them out but other times I do not.

Lyndsay Swinton gives tips on how to set SMART goals and I think you need to pay rapt attention to them. SMART stands for **S**pecific, **M**easurable, **A**chievable, **R**elevant and **T**ime-bound, and is a useful reminder of how to write a top-quality goal. Here's what it means...

i. **Specific** – your goal should have its expected outcome stated as simply, concisely and explicitly as possible. This answers questions such as; how much, for whom, for what?
ii. **Measurable** – a measurable goal has an outcome that can be assessed either on a sliding scale (1-10) or as a hit or miss, success or failure.
iii. **Achievable** – an achievable goal has an outcome that is realistic given your current situation, resources and time available. Goal achievement may be more of a "stretch" if the outcome is tough or you have a weak starting position.
iv. **Relevant** – a relevant goal should help you on your mission or your "bigger" objectives.
v. **Time-bound** – a time-bound goal includes realistic timeframes.[57]

---

[57]Lyndsay Swinton. *Goal Setting Guide,* (United Kingdom: Uncommon Knowledge Ltd, 2006), 4.

Even though I knew less about systematically setting goals at the time I was getting married, I could still set my goals as to relating my wedding and I married on a set day. After so many years of marriage, I stumbled upon my wedding plan file and it was exciting. It looked as if I was not the person that did the entire plan back then.

I tell you the truth; planning a wedding almost all by myself was one of the most difficult and challenging tasks in my life at the time. I bought the cheapest wedding ring that was available in town. My friend Tersoo, who gave me the wedding suit only arrived on the morning of the day of the wedding. The wedding did not start until 1:00 pm. But the most important thing for me as regarding my wedding was that I married the woman I loved at the date I set, with the finances that were available.

Scoring your goals is tantamount to setting your goals. When you set your goals, you can definitely score them. In the game of soccer, all players aim towards a specific direction where they can score. The players in a particular team do all they can to score goals. Scoring a goal is a deliberately planned endeavour. Hard work and planning is involved, but the starting point is at the point of setting them.

Could it be that the reason you may not be succeeding in life is you aim at nothing? I have told you that when you aim at nothing, you get nothing. Your attitude towards your dreams can turn around if you begin to plan and set goals about anything and everything you do. Take the cue from other successful people in life; be creative, be the goal setter and the goal-getter.

Do not forget, the law of creativity has its strength in thinking, and great ideas do not just come by, it takes diligence. You will be better off if you cultivate the habit of writing your ideas down. You need to know, however, as good as this law is, it is useless without the second law, which is commitment.

5. Law two: Commitment

I've failed over and over and
over again in my life and that
is why I succeed.
-**Michael Jordan**

T HE FIRST LAW OF SUCCESS WHICH IS creativity is a great law. Its shortcoming is that; it cannot work independently of the second law. We do not live in a dream world, therefore, no matter what you think and must have written down, a-well-thought-out-plan is useless without implementation.

The law of commitment is what brings your action into reality. Commitment takes a lot of discipline, and an undisciplined and uncommitted person is a double-minded person who will find it difficult to fulfill his or her goals. To properly align with what commitment is all about, a definition will be appropriate at this point.

Commitment defined

The Cambridge dictionary online defines commitment as, "a willingness to give your time and energy to something that you believe in, or a promise or firm decision to do something"[58] A person who lacks commitment is of a double mind and unstable. The life manual says of such a person that, *"[For being as he is] a man of two minds (hesitating, dubious, irresolute), [he is] unstable and unreliable and uncertain about everything [he thinks, feels, decides]."*[59]

To be committed therefore requires focus. It takes to the Spartan law "no retreat, no surrender". Commitment, therefore, is the second principle of the Loho-u-Ter breakthrough strategy which goes thus:

I believe that any individual that is committed to his or her ideas and goals is on the way to achievement.

---

[58] Cambridge Dictionary, Definition of commitment," [cited August 18, 2015] Online: http://dictionary.cambridge.org/dictionary/english/commitment.
[59] James 1:8. Amplified Bible.

This law has its base in a quote of the life manual which says, *"He becomes poor that deals with a slack hand: but the hand of the diligent makes rich."*[60] A committed person must never be slack or lazy. We will be looking at the different twists of commitment to help us take full advantage of commitment to be committed.

a.   Commitment is action

Action is simply the process of doing something. No matter your strategy to achieve a goal, without taking the needed action, your plans are useless. You need to meet some guys; they are all the ideas you dream about. Most of their ideas are a million-dollar idea, but they are still in the dirt because they have not made the move to implement their ideas.

Since I started writing, I have discovered that many people are authors. The challenge is most of them are still in the dream world. Some told me they have been thinking of writing, others have developed an outline, while others have started writing or haven't finished writing.

---

[60] Proverbs 10:4. King James Version.

I have met great men who have written books so many years ago. I met a minister of God who has written as many as five books. I met another young man who told me he has written ten books, but years have passed without even one of these books being published. What is the point of spending so much time, resources, and energy to write a book that is accumulating dust on your shelf or is neatly tuck under your box? Commitment is action. The ability to act starts with a step. Do not allow your wonderful ideas to lay fallow. Take the action and put your creativity to use.

b. Commitment is service

I strongly believe that all human beings were created primarily for three things. We are created for:

i. The glory of God
ii. Relationships
iii. Service.

I hope you have not forgotten Maxwell's definition of success which is, "knowing your purpose in life, growing to reach your maximum potential, and sowing seeds that benefit others."[61] The seed that

---

[61] Maxwell. *Your road map for success,* 11.

benefits others can be called service. Service is the action of helping or doing work for someone else to the glory of God.

When you are committed to serving others, you develop the potentials to be the best at what you do. Your experience in the service to people comes handy on a rainy day. More so, your maker blesses you for the service you render to others and he says. *"Whoever can be trusted with a little can also be trusted with a lot, and whoever is dishonest with a little is dishonest with a lot... if you cannot be trusted with things that belong to someone else, who will give you things of your own?"*[62]

Your ability to serve others helps you to be committed to your goals. If you must succeed with your purpose for life. Service to others is the key that trains and helps you to commit yourself to your goals.

c. Commitment is concentration

To concentrate is to direct one's attention to a specific object. I bet that there are a thousand and one conflicting interests that exist to make you lose

---

[62] Luke 16:10,12. New Century Version.

focus on your goals. If you do not learn and develop the power of concentration, people and events will always suggest a very big distraction to you.

Some people are finding it difficult to make headway in life because they are rather concentrating on the failures of the past or a painful experience that has now become an obstacle to their progress. If you do not take charge of your life, limiting circumstances will engulf you and put a halt to your success progress. James Allen says:

> Man is buffeted by circumstances so long as he believes himself to be the creature of outside conditions, but when he realizes that he is a creative power, and that he may command the hidden soil and seeds of his being out of which circumstances grow; he then becomes the rightful master of himself.[63]

Taking charge of yourself helps you concentrate on what you want to think. You should rather think about the things that would bring you joy and success and not the limiting thoughts. Robbins advises that you can change the channel if what you

---

[63] James Allen, *As a man thinketh*, (St. Augustine: AsAManThinketh.net, 2001), 9.

are focusing on is bringing you pain, and he says, "You've got to focus on what empowers you. Whatever you focus on—whatever you tune in to— you will feel more intensely. So if you don't like what you're doing, maybe it's time to change the channel."[64] He further says:

> There are unlimited sensations, unlimited ways of looking at virtually anything in life. All of the sensations that you want are available all of the time, and all you've got to do is to tune in to the right channel. There are two primary ways, then, to change your emotional state: by changing the way you use your physical body, or by changing your focus.[65]

You have a goal to succeed in life, isn't it? You have an idea or a project you want to accomplish? Then you should redirect your focus, be committed to making sure that you achieve your goals.

Sometimes you will have to put sleep, food, and every kind of fun on hold in order to concentrate on some specific goals which must be achieved within a specific time. If your purpose means so much to you,

---

[64] Robbins. *Awaken the giant within,* 155.
[65] Robbins. *Awaken the giant within,* 155.

focus on it, for whatever you concentrate on becomes your idea of reality.[66]

d.   Commitment is risk-taking

The likelihood of a negative outcome is what is called risk. Our everyday life is full of risks, and no matter how you want to avoid risk, it still knocks at your door. The most we can do is to reduce risk as much as it depends on us.

Robert Toru Kiyosaki, an American businessman, investor, self-help author, motivational speaker, financial literacy activist, financial commentator, and radio personality. Is the founder of the Rich Dad Company who has gone through various risks in his climb to financial wealth, who also says:

> Life is full of risk. We don't totally control—much as we'd like to think we do. But we can reduce the risk and increase our leverage by becoming educated, making moderate choices and keeping a positive attitude. A lot of people have been great successes when the supposed "odds" were entirely against them. They won because they

---

[66] Robbins. *Awaken the giant within,* 160.

decided to take control of their destiny and refused to give up.[67]

A person that chickens out of his or her goals is mediocre and can hardly succeed. In Kiyosaki's experience, he has identified that people of great successes are the ones that do not give up in the midst of risks. No investment in this life is without risk. Tracy also says "Risk is inherent in any investment of time, money, or emotions."[68] You cannot say because you went to some church and it was a complete waste of time, you will stop going to church. You cannot say because you invested money in some business and the deal did not yield, you will stop investing. And you cannot say because you were in a relationship to be married and your lover broke your heart, you would never get married. Life is full of risks and it only takes the courageous to break even.

Do your research and find out, the most successful people in the world, are those who are courageous enough to take risks. For such people, their names

---

[67] Donald J. Trump and Robert T. Kiyosaki. *Why we want you to be rich*, (New York: Rich Press, 2006), 137.
[68] Tracy. *The 100Absoluetely unbreakable law of business success*, 208.

are written in gold. Check this out, the story of three risk-takers and what they did for the sake of their king:

Once when David was at the rock near the cave of Adullam, the Philistine army was camped in the valley of Rephaim. The Three (who were among the Thirty—an elite group among David's fighting men) went down to meet him there. David was staying in the stronghold at the time, and a Philistine detachment had occupied the town of Bethlehem.

David remarked longingly to his men, "Oh, how I would love some of that good water from the well by the gate in Bethlehem." So the Three broke through the Philistine lines, drew some water from the well by the gate in Bethlehem, and brought it back to David. But David refused to drink it. Instead, he poured it out as an offering to the LORD. "God forbid that I should drink this!" he exclaimed. "This water is as precious as the blood of these men who risked their lives to bring it to me." So David did not drink it. These are examples of the exploits of the Three.[69]

These three mighty men took the risk to activate their courage-mode in the time of great danger and did what the whole army would have been scared of doing. Winston Churchill once said, "Courage is rightly considered the foremost of the virtues, for upon it, all others depend."[70] In the midst of risks, dare to be committed by grasping the bull by the horns, induce the ability to make decisions and act boldly in the face of setbacks and adversity. This attitude is what courage is and it is a key to greatness.[71]

e.   Commitment is tolerance

No matter how cool you'll want to be, there are some people who are difficult to tolerate. It can be even worse if your path to success crosses such people. Some of these people have simply made themselves unlikable. They are arrogant, bossy, sarcastic, impossible, bullies, and extortionists. If it were

---

[69] 1 Chronicles 11:15-19. New Living Translation.
[70] Tracy. *The 100Absoluetely unbreakable law of business success,* 123.
[71] Tracy. *The 100Absoluetely unbreakable law of business success,* 123.

possible, you would want to do all you can to avoid them.

There are also situations that you find yourself in, that are almost unbearable. There are people who do the most demeaning jobs. They know exactly where they are going but circumstances have landed them where they are right now.

I know of a young man who had a master's degree but because he had no other job, he resorted to being a taxi driver, but today he is lecturing in a university. He did not lose hope in life when he was a taxi driver. I know another young man who was hawking bread to pay his school fees in the university but today he has his degree and is happy with his current job.

A committed person will envision the future and disregard the unpleasant situation he or she is currently going through. To, therefore, achieve your set goals, you have to tolerate people and situations to focus on what you want to achieve in life.

f.   Commitment is integrity

Your value increases when you are a person of integrity. Value can be money. The more your value increases, the richer you will become. A person of integrity is said to be a person who steadfastly adheres to strict moral or ethical codes. I had once read somewhere that a person of integrity is the one who does what he or she says he or she will do.

I would not claim to be perfect but I do my best to be a person of integrity. I remember when I was invited to conduct a seminar somewhere in Benue state, and another group wanted me to facilitate a seminar in Port Harcourt on the same date. The meeting in Port Harcourt was likely to bring me more money, and it was at a time I really needed some extra cash. The temptation to go to Port Harcourt was very high but I had given the organization whose seminar was taking place in Benue state my word. Once I made up my mind, I told the organization in Port Harcourt to make arrangements for another facilitator and I immediately had my peace. The program coordinator and the national coordinator of this organization were pleased that I kept my word to honour the Benue meeting with my presence.

When you want to reach your goals in life, you will need to be a person of your word. You must be a person of integrity. You must be committed to your values. This is one commitment (Commitment to integrity) that many people are found wanting. You can dare to be different by showing yourself worthy. You can dare to be that person of integrity no matter the cost.

g.   Commitment is affirmation

Scott Armstrong says affirmations are, "you being in conscious control of your thoughts. They are short, powerful statements. When you say them or think them or even hear them, they become the thoughts that create your reality. Affirmations, then, are your conscious thoughts."[72] Similarly, Remez Sasson says:

Affirmations are sentences aimed to affect the conscious and the subconscious mind. The words composing the affirmation, automatically and involuntarily, bring up related mental images into the mind, which could inspire, energize and motivate. Repeating affirmations, and the resultant mental images, affect the subconscious

---

[72] Boulder Coaching Academy, "Affirmation," [cited August 21, 2015] Online:
http://www.bouldercoachingacademy.com/affirmations/what -is-an-affirmation-they-will-change-your-life-forever/

mind, which in turn, influences the behavior, habits, actions, and reactions.[73]

Affirmations motivate; they keep the mind focused on the goal, they influence the subconscious mind and activate its powers, they change the way you think and behave, and this can bring you into contact with new people, who can help you with your goals. Positive statements make you feel positive, energetic and active, and therefore, put you in a better position to transform your inner and external worlds.[74]

My daughter Sharon says her best Bollywood movie is *"The Three Idiots."* Her key actor is Ranchhoddas Shamaldas Chanchas simply called Ranchos. Sharon does not consider him an idiot. Ranchos has a wonderful way of affirmation. He will always say "Aal izz well" in times of trouble and when he needs to be courageous to face his fears. In many cases, he gently taps his right hand on the position of the heart in the course of affirmation. Aamir Khan who starred in the Movie as Ranchos experienced a lot of

---

[73] Success Consciousness, "Affirmation," [cited August 21, 2015] Online:
http://www.successconsciousness.com/affirmations.htm.
[74] Success Consciousness, "Affirmation," (cited 21 August, 2015).

challenges but he kept telling himself "Aal izz well"—All is well, and things went well with him. His simple philosophy of life was this: "follow excellence... Success will chase you." With courage and affirmation, he confronted his challenges and emerged victorious at the end of the movie.

Affirmations are great, but they are not the solution to challenges, especially if they do not come along with questions, and are not focused. Robbins says:

> When you say to yourself, "I'm happy; I'm happy; I'm happy," this might cause you to feel happy if you produce enough emotional intensity, change your physiology and therefore your state. But in reality, you can make affirmations all day long and not really change how you feel.[75]

Now! When you are affirming, ask questions like, "What am I happy about now? What could I be happy about if I wanted to be? How would that make me feel?"[76] Robbins says, "If you keep asking questions like this, you will come up with real references that will make you begin to focus on

---

[75] Robbins. *Awaken the giant within*, 186.
[76] Robbins. *Awaken the giant within*, 186.

reasons that do in fact exist for you to feel happy. You'll feel certain that you're happy."

So instead of just pumping yourself up with empty affirmations, incorporate questions in your mind as you do your affirmations. Ask reasonable questions that will point you in the right direction. "Questions provide you with actual reasons to feel the emotion. You and I can change how we feel in an instant, just by changing our focus."[77]

The Evolution Team suggests that "For affirmations to be truly effective, they need to be repeated frequently throughout the day – or even better, on an ongoing basis for longer periods of time."[78] When I have a goal ahead of me, I tell myself, "Shadrach you can do this." And in my mind, I try to figure out what to do. I picture myself doing what I ought to do. I commit myself to the big picture and concentrate on all I need to do to get there no matter the odds. And in most cases, I get there.

---

[77] Robbins. *Awaken the giant within*, 186.
[78] Evolution Team and Evolution Readers, "22 Powerful Tools to Transform Your Fear into Happiness, Peace and Inspiration," [cited August 18, 2019] Online: www.FreeFromFear.com and www.EvolutionEzine.com

Affirmations can take various forms depending on the situation you find yourself in. I used to hear my father constantly say, "I can do all things through Christ who strengthens me." My friend Godwin Oboatsaga of blessed memory will constantly say, "Lord, help your little boy." He believed that God would help him and he of course did. Create your affirmation with the picture of your goal in your mind, and commit yourself to it, for no affirmation works properly without your commitment and focus on the big picture.

h.   Commitment is relationship

No matter how good you are at what you do, at some point you will need someone to give you a helping hand. It is, therefore, important to have good relationships that are capable of being the extra hand you need to achieve your goals. It is unfortunate, however, that some people find it difficult to associate with others as a result of their attitude.

A bad attitude can kill a long-standing friendship and hinder you from making new ones, so do not take your relationships for granted by exhibiting a bad attitude. For example, do not crack coarse jokes that are capable of ruining your relationships. Your mouth can cut you away from a relationship that would have made you wealthy. Michael Lee especially warns that you should think first before you speak, for:

Many relationships have been ruined by the wrong choice of words. Some people voice out anything that comes to their mind, without first filtering the good words from the bad ones. This might result in misunderstandings and arguments, which could have easily been prevented if we speak out in a way that is neutral and non- offensive. Words are very powerful indeed. Use them responsibly for the benefit of all.[79]

Maintaining good relationships gives you the leverage you need to be committed to your vision. Kiyosaki takes advantage of his relationships to get the desired leverage he needs to achieve his goals, and he says:

Once you understand leverage, which is the ability to do more with less, you will probably begin to see leverage everywhere. For example, the chair I am sitting on is a form of leverage. It

---

[79] Michael Lee, *21 Powerful Ways to Persuade People to Do What You Want,* (www.20daypersuasion.com), 39.

would be tough for me to sit on the ground and type with ease. Having partners is a leverage. At The Rich Dad Company. I combine my talents with Kim's and Sharon's talents which gives me more leverage than working on my own...[80]

It is unfortunate, however, that many people do not take advantage of their relationships to be the leverage both of them can enjoy. The boss wants the be the solo boss, the pastor wants to be the solo pastor, the married want to do things on their own apart from their spouses, and many business people suffer needlessly because they do not understand how to get the desired leverage they need to succeed in their relationships.

Kiyosaki further says:

Leverage can come in many forms. Leverage can be your thoughts. People who win are careful with their thoughts. They don't think to themselves. "I can't do that." Or it's too risky." Or, "I can't afford it" Instead they think. "How can I

---

[80] Donald J. Trump and Robert T. Kiyosaki. *Why we want you to be rich*, (New York: Rich Press, 2006), 131.

do that?" Or, "How can I reduce my risk?" Or, "How can I afford it?"[81]

I am not necessarily discussing leverage at this point but I am saying you need people in your life to get the leverage you must. This will help you achieve your goals faster. Enter the world of billionaires like Kiyosakis' and the Trumps' and see how they use leverage. Kiyosaki even says that "Rich people use more leverage than poor people."[82] And that, "If you want to be rich, you need leverage. If you want to be really rich, you need a lot of leverage."[83]

I am certain you would not want to fail. If you really want to succeed, pay attention to your family relationships, your colleagues, your business partners, your marriage, and every other relationship you are in for you don't know whose leverage you'll need to get to your desired goals.

i. Commitment is motivation

No matter how much you are motivated by external forces, at some point you will need to be personally motivated to carry on with your life. Kate Burton and

---

[81] Trump and Kiyosaki. *Why we want you to be rich*, 131.
[82] Trump and Kiyosaki. *Why we want you to be rich*, 131.
[83] Trump and Kiyosaki. *Why we want you to be rich*, 131.

Brinley Platts in their book *Building Confidence for Dummies* say, "Your personal motivation is the force that gets you out of bed in the morning and provides you with energy for the work of the day. Have you ever wondered why you seem to be bursting with it some days, and other times it seems to desert you entirely?"[84]

If you do not learn to be personally motivated, the pressures of life will force you to assume the position of a pessimist or worrywart. Burton and Platts say, "The more motivated you feel the more inclined you are to push yourself through the things that are holding you back. If you can increase your motivation, you automatically increase your confidence."[85]

Many people are hardly motivated because of their self-confidence. Their self-image is one of their biggest challenges in life. In many cases, they feel like trash because of what they have done or experienced in the past, or because of their height,

---

[84]Kate Burton and Brinley Platts. *Building Confidence for Dummies,* (West Sussex: John Wiley & Sons, Ltd, 2006), 51.
[85] Kate Burton and Brinley Platts. *Building Confidence for Dummies,* 51.

ethnicity, complexion, or what they assume is beauty.

Friend! You are one unique person who is not made to fit in but stand out. Do not let anyone define who you are. They have no idea how you were formed. Job understood who should define him and said of the creator:

> Your hands shaped and made me... You formed me inside my mother like cheese formed from milk. You dressed me with skin and flesh; you sewed me together with bones and muscles. You gave me life and showed me kindness, and in your care, you watched over my life.[86]

Your maker could not have made a mistake by creating you the way you are. He knows why he made you the way you are. People may even associate a deformity to you, or have a bizarre impression about the way you are formed. But that is their definition and not Gods.

---

[86] Job 10:8,10-12. New Century Version.

David Lawrence Preston says Your self-image—the way you see yourself is made up of three core feelings and beliefs:

i.   Self-worth: the value you place on yourself – how comfortable you are at being you and the extent to which you feel worthy of happiness and success.

ii. Competence: your beliefs about your capacity to achieve, solve problems and think for yourself. This is what I mean by confidence.

iii. Belonging: whether you feel accepted and respected by others[87].

Self-worth, competence, and your associations can be enhanced and improved if you know who you are, what stock you are made of, and who should define you. King David understood this fact and knew who should define him and he said:

Thank you for making me so wonderfully complex! Your workmanship is marvelous—how well I know it. You watched me as I was being formed in utter seclusion, as I was woven together in the dark of the womb. You saw me before I was born. Every day of my life was

---

[87]David Lawrence Preston. *360 steps to Self-confidence,* (Oxford: How to book LTD, 2001), 18.

recorded in your book. Every moment was laid out before a single day had passed. How precious are your thoughts about me, O God. They cannot be numbered! I can't even count them; they outnumber the grains of sand! And when I wake up, you are still with me![88]

Your maker defines who you are, so get up and get motivated. You may sometimes need to get external help to keep you motivated. A good movie, a book, attending a seminar, going to church, listening to music, talking with your loved one if you are married; sex can also get you motivated. Whatever gets you motivated to stay committed to your goals is okay, as long as it does not violate the purpose to which you were made—to glorify God, for healthy relationships, and for true service.

j.   Commitment is priority

No one is free from multiple activities. Achieving your goals may require you to do several things at the same time, but are all the things we get involved with priority? How far can we go in achieving our purpose by doing too much? The result will be fatigue, stress,

---

[88]Psalm 139:14-18. New Living Translation.

and burnout. The Eisenhower's Urgent/Important Principle helps us to prioritize our activities.

Sarah Pavey and the Mind Tools Team tries to give a history on how the Eisenhower's Urgent/Important Principle originated and they say:

> In a 1954 speech to the Second Assembly of the World Council of Churches, former U.S. President Dwight D. Eisenhower, who was quoting Dr J. Roscoe Miller, president of Northwestern University, said: "I have two kinds of problems: the urgent and the important. The urgent are not important, and the important are never urgent."[89]

Dwight D. Eisenhower used this principle to organize his workload and priorities. Pavey and the Mind Tools Team gives an idea on the Eisenhower's Urgent/Important Principle. But you have to be honest with yourself and others to be able to put your priorities right.

---

[89] Sarah Pavey and the Mind Tools Team, "Eisenhower's Urgent/Important Principle," [cited August 21, 2015] Online: http://www.mindtools.com/pages/article/newHTE_91.htm.

i. *Important and Urgent activities*

There are two distinct types of urgent and important activities: ones that you could not have foreseen, and others that you've left until the last minute.

You can eliminate last-minute activities by planning ahead and avoiding procrastination.

ii. *Important but Not Urgent activities*

These are the activities that help you achieve your personal and professional goals and complete important work.

iii. *Not Important but Urgent activities*

Urgent but not important tasks are things that prevent you from achieving your goals. Ask yourself whether you can reschedule or delegate them.

iv. *Not Important and not Urgent activities*

These activities are just a distraction – avoid them if possible. You can simply ignore or cancel many of them. However, some may be activities that other people want you to do, even though they don't contribute to your own desired outcomes. Again, say "no" politely, if you can, and explain why you cannot do it. [90]

Commitment without prioritizing is tantamount to a waste of time. You should at all times have your goals at the back of your mind. Yes, you can have fun, you can enjoy a movie, and you can hang out with friends, but never allow someone to cajole you into doing something because you do not want to disappoint him or her at the detriment of your success goals. Your goals should be your urgent and important activities. They should be at the top of your priorities timetable. That is how a person who is committed to success should live his or her life.

---

[90] The Eisenhower's Urgent/Important Principle presented here is abridged by me to fit my context.
Pavey and the Mind Tools Team, "Eisenhower's Urgent/Important Principle," (cited 21 August, 2015).

6. Law three: Consistency

The difference between a
successful person and others
is not a lack of strength, not a
lack of knowledge, but rather
a lack of will.
-Vince Lombardi

THE THIRD LAW OF SUCCESS IS consistency. Consistency could mean different things to different people. A look at the Merriam-Webster dictionary gives one an idea about what it means to be consistent:

i. To be consistent means possessing firmness or coherence

ii. a. Consistency is marked by harmony, regularity, or steady continuity: free from variation or contradiction.

b. Marked by agreement: compatibility—usually used with <statements not consistent with truth>

    c. Showing steady conformity to character, profession, belief, or custom < consistent patriot>

  iii. To be consistent is tending to be arbitrarily close to the true value of a parameter estimated as the sample becomes large.[91]

If I may ask. What can you be associated with? What do people easily identify you for doing? Are you here today and there tomorrow? Do you start one business; the next moment you are dumping it for what people seem to suggest to you? How then can you gain mastery about anything that will yield the needed fruit in the pursuit of your goals without being consistent?

To be consistent is to be truthful and hold firm to success goals. Sometimes life is very discouraging, especially when what you are doing does not seem to yield timely fruits in line with your expectations. To be consistent is related to regularity, its other synonyms are steadiness, reliability, evenness, uniformity, and stability. My guiding light to this principle is based on a quote in the life manual which says. *"For the vision is yet for an appointed time, but*

---

[91] Meaning of consistent is from Merriam-Webster dictionary. Android application 2015. n.p.

at the end, it shall speak, and not lie: though it tarry, wait for it; because it will surely come, it will not tarry."[92] The principle itself says:

> *I believe that any individual that is committed and consistent with achieving his or her goals no matter the tides and storms of life will surely attain them to the maximum.*

One of the greatest challenges to a successful life is the ability to stay consistent. To be successful is to get a breakthrough in your success goals. Imagine for instance, that your goal is to reach the other side of a certain rock and it is not possible to walk around it, beneath it, or over it. The only choice left is to go through or break through the rock. If it were a spider web that was your obstacle, you could just walk through it. Unfortunately, breakthrough is not walk-through. It takes time and deliberate hard work to achieve a breakthrough.

I have often taught in my seminars that there are two ways to break through your obstacle—You either have the energy that is mightier than your obstacle— If you do, you can generate a force and hit your blockade with a mightier force to break through to

---

[92] Habakkuk 2:3 King James Version.

your success goals—Or, you will chisel through your obstacle gradually until you finally breakthrough to your goals.

The ability to think of chiseling through the rock is creativity, the energy to chisel is commitment, and the power to stay on till you breakthrough is consistency. But since it is not always very clear when you will breakthrough, you will be required to be consistent in pursuing your goals until you get your consummation.

Many people were just a few inches to their breakthrough when they decided to quit. They made statements like, "this thing is not working and I have put so much money and energy into it, let me better look for something that works." Can you imagine having a grocery store—supermarket, and after operating for a year, you can barely pay your staff and you quit? There is another guy down the road in a more disadvantaged location doing the same business of selling groceries, who has been committed and consistent with his for three years. This person has discovered how to get commodities at a cheaper rate and the nitty-gritties of the business but has been looking for a better location, then all of a sudden you vacated your store to go look for so-called greener pastures. The person now moves into the store you were occupying and reaps the effort you have put in in the last year because people that used to buy from you will keep coming to the same location. Customers that used to buy from him or her will be directed to his or her new location, and the person will reap from your labour of a whole year because of you quite.

If you have discovered your purpose in life, or you have decided to be wealthy, or successful in any area of life, set your goals and stick to them. Things may not always go as you planned. But remember, everything about life is risky, and good things in most cases do not come so easily. Winners do not quit especially when they are sure they on the right track. The consistent always win, while the "neither-here-nor-there" are always complaining as to why they are not making any headway.

People are too polite to tell you the truth. They will tell you God's time is the best, but I will not hide the truth from you. If you are not consistent with your goals, you can never get a breakthrough no matter how good your idea is. People will always reap from your ideas. You will be what they say in my country. "Monkey dey work, baboon dey chop."—the monkey is working but is the baboon that enjoys the fruit of his labour. You can work and enjoy the fruit of your labour by being creative, committed, and consistent. It is then that your consummation—breakthrough will come.

a.   Consistency is improvement

There is a saying in my language, "ahi nga hier or apir ashe atsenge ahar ga"—a blind man that burnt his groundnuts in the first instant of roasting; will get it right at the second attempt. This meant the blind person learn from experience that since the groundnut burnt at the first instant, he would start tasting at an earlier stage to determine if it is ready.

It is only a stupid person that keeps doing something over and over without a shred of improvement. Consistency gives birth to improvement. Have you not heard that "practice makes perfect?" When you keep doing stuff over and over, there is a tendency that you would be better as compared with when you first began.

When I started writing, I made a lot of blunders. I could even quote without acknowledging the source. In writing, that act is called plagiarism—the act of using another person's words or ideas without giving credit to that person.[93] I don't do that anymore because I have improved.

When you are consistent with anything, you know the pros and cons of the thing. You become a professional in it. I guess that is why it takes a long time to be a medical doctor, because of the value placed on human life. Because of this value, the leaders in the medical profession will want the medical students to keep practicing on the nitty gritty of the human body before attempting to bring solutions to its challenges.

I understand that in medical school, students are exposed to lifeless bodies to practice surgery before they are exposed to real human beings, but with strict supervision. The medical student through consistent studies and practice finally gains mastery on how to handle sick people. Even then, the longer a person stays in the medical profession or any other profession, the person becomes better.

What makes you stand out in your endeavours is how consistent you have been in improving what you do. People who did not believe in you when you started

---

[93] Merriam-Webster dictionary. Android application 2015. n.p.

will marvel at your improvement and will want to identify with you because you have been consistent. Believe me, success attracts.

When you are a better you or have improved from when you started, people who looked down on you will look up to you for help. Some people are waiting to see your seriousness before they can be of help to you. Do not blame them. They have invested their time, energy, and money in great ideas that never yielded fruits, and so they are more careful in order not to invest in a venture that may turn up to be worthless like the others.

If you are doing one thing over and over, and you are not improving, it is most likely that it is not your purpose in life and therefore, your interest is not ignited. Please do not waste your time on any venture that does not ignite your interest because the likelihood for you to improve is very slim. But if something ignites your interest and you seem to be improving, keep at it, be consistent, and your improvement will come.

b. Consistency is persistence

It is when you persist on your goals that the needed improvement will come. When you persevere, it means you must have also failed several times. Because you failed today does not make you a failure. Failure is part of the process of success. Yes, you have failed and so what? Dust yourself from the ground and get up, learn from people who have failed like Abraham Lincoln and get to your success goals.

Lincoln in:

1831 - Lost his job

1832 - Defeated in run for Illinois State Legislature

1833 - Failed in business

1834 - Elected to Illinois State Legislature (**success**)

1835 - Sweetheart died

1836 - Had nervous breakdown

1838 - Defeated in run for Illinois House Speaker

1843 - Defeated in run for nomination for U.S. Congress

1846 - Elected to Congress (**success**)

1848 - Lost re-nomination

1849 - Rejected for land officer position

1854 - Defeated in run for U.S. Senate

1856 - Defeated in run for nomination for Vice President

1858 - Again defeated in run for U.S. Senate

1860 - Elected President (**success**)[94]

He did not quit on life because he failed several times. He would always pick himself up and persevere, he did persevere until he reached his consummation—breakthrough. So, if you thought you have failed and that is it, then you better think again. Failure is a process of success. The difference between a mediocre and a successful person is that the other quit in the midst of failure; while the other persevered even though they failed over and over along the way.

Bob Bastian says, "To reach your success, you need to persevere. Even Thomas Edison had to learn this. When he was creating the incandescent light bulb, it took him more than 10,000 times to get it right. Keep striving even when it becomes challenging.[95] Wow! 10,000 times? How many of us can persevere to this extent? The bulk of what you enjoy today is the labour of people who persevered until they got to their success goals. Why do you not persevere in your

---

[94]Ron Kurtu. "Failures of Abraham Lincoln (1800s)," [cited August 18, 2018] Online: http://www.school-for-champions.com/history/lincoln_failures

[95] Bob Bastian. *404 improvement tips,* (Sumatera Selatan: Bob Bastian and omniwebmarketing.com, 2004), 35

success goals so that people will remember you for what you have contributed to humanity? The world awaits you, keep hanging in there. Your day of manifestation is closer than when you first started.

c. Consistency is staying focused

People quit because their eyes are somewhere else apart from their goals. You see young people go to school to obtain a certificate. One will think that they know that their primary goal in school is to attend classes, read their books, and pass their exams. But it marvels me that out of the 24 hours they have in a day, some will spend less than four hours for both their classes and reading. The rest of the hours are spent on chatting on the net, hanging out with their boy or girlfriends, going to parties, sleeping, and just idling around.

Students who lose focus on what took them to school will hardly succeed. Some business persons who suddenly changed their lifestyle because some few millions came in, and have stopped focusing on his or her success goals will cry at the end.

At no time in life should you forget what you were created for. Focus on your goals in life that will take you to your success goals. If possible, read your life goals out loud to yourself every day. Also read out goals for a particular project you are undertaking. Your goals should be your compass in the right direction.

The most powerful man that ever lived could walk on water, calm storms, and could do all manner of miracles. One day, this son of man was walking on water, and one of his associates asked permission to also walk on water and the permission was granted, and wow! He also began to walk on water as long as his focus was on his master. The life manual records that:

> ...Jumping out of the boat, Peter walked on the water to Jesus. But when he looked down at the waves churning beneath his feet, he lost his nerve and started to sink. He cried, "Master, save me!" Jesus didn't hesitate. He reached down and grabbed his hand. Then he said, "Faint-heart, what got into you?" [96]

Peter began to sink because he lost focus and began to look at the challenging waves. Lack of focus can induce fear in the midst of storms. But when you focus on your goals and your attention is always

---

[96] Mathew 14:29-31. The Message.

there, the energy to keep at it will be induced by your maker through the force that is in you.

When I got the clarity of my purpose and decided to leave Jos for Benue state as at then, many friends felt that I should stay. One organization that my wife was working with really wanted me to stay and sent one of their staff to talk me into staying. They were willing to give me a job in the organization and my wife a house loan so we could stay, but I refused. The delegate that was asked to talk me into staying scheduled a meeting with me, and I came along with my laptop. After showing him the PowerPoint of my vision and the reason why I need to leave Jos as at that time, he said. "You know exactly what you are doing." Of a truth, at that stage of my life, I knew where my focus was.

When you are not focused on your goals, people will know and assume you do not know what you are doing. They will get you involved in all manner of chores. I have seen a lot of young people wasting around their spiritual leaders. Your leader knows when you do not have goals and a direction in life. A good leader will help you to discover who you are, a bad leader will use you to accomplish his or her goals and dump you like trash.

You may not have achieved your success goals yet. But if you keep at your goals, people will respect you for keeping to those goals, even if they do not understand, with time, you will gain the mastery that will take you to where you want to go and then they will understand.

d.   Consistency is expectations

A person who goes into a business or any venture with the mind-set of past failures will hardly reach his or her success goals. "Whatever you expect, with confidence, becomes your own self-fulfilling prophecy."[97] The dictionary definition of expectation is a belief that something will happen or is likely to happen, or a feeling or belief about how successful, good, etc., someone or something will be."[98]

It is the hope or expectation of success that keeps any person active, as they strive to accomplish their mission. When hope is lost, the energy to forge ahead dissipates. The staying power to your mission is the hope that success will come. Expectation keeps a

---

[97] Tracy. *The 100Absoluetely unbreakable law of business success*, 19.
[98] Meaning of expectation is from Merriam-Webster dictionary. Android application 2015. n.p.

person through difficult situations that the ordinary weakling must have quitted. The expectant will stop at nothing until their success goals are achieved. Paul the tent-maker wrote a letter to his compatriots at Rome to keep their hopes high on the better life and he said:

> Moreover [let us also be full of joy now!] let us exult and triumph in our troubles and rejoice in our sufferings, knowing that pressure and affliction and hardship produce patient and unswerving endurance. And endurance (fortitude) develops maturity of character (approved faith and tried integrity). And character [of this sort] produces [the habit of] joyful and confident hope...[99]And this hope will not lead to disappointment...[100]

Are you already getting disappointed that things are not going the way you planned? Please be hopeful. If you had set your goals right. The things you are going through are there to help build you and sharpen your expectations. Remember what the tent maker said in the quote above, *"pressure and affliction and hardship produce patient and*

---

[99] Romans 5:3-4. Amplified Bible.
[100] Romans 5:5. New Living Translation.

unswerving endurance. And endurance (fortitude) develops maturity of character (approved faith and tried integrity). And character [of this sort] produces [the habit of] joyful and confident hope..."

A person that stops expecting will lose the nerve to be committed and consistent with his or her goals. So I want to tell you that all hope is not lost until you succeed. Even if you seem to be down right now, it is part of the process of getting to your success goals. Would you just allow all the efforts you have put into your pursuit of success to go just like that? I do not think so. So keep working hard with expectations.

e.   Consistency is control

Control is to have power over something or to be on top of the situation. One valuable asset to get to your success goals is time. When your time is not managed well, there is a tendency for failure. In view of this, Ann Marie Sabath asked the following questions.

i.   Do you plan your work and then work your plan?
ii. Do you act rather than react?

iii. Do you manage interruptions rather than letting them manage you? [101]

When you do not properly take charge of your time, getting to your goals becomes a challenge. You just end up reacting to situations. Talking about time management, Ann says:

> Effective time managers create a daily list of what they want to accomplish. Whether they have a block of 10 minutes or an hour, they refer to their to-do list to see what, exactly, they can accomplish. They also plan their "prime time"— the time of day that they are most likely to be able to "act" rather than "react." [102]

My prime time is usually at night. There was a time I was awoken by a phone call at about 9:00 am, and the person asked. "Are you still sleeping at this time of the day?" I almost asked, "Do you know the time of the day I slept?" But I just maintained my cool.

The nature of what you do will determine your prime time. My prime time is from 2:00 am to 6:00 am. But

---

[101] Ann Marie Sabath. *BUSINESS ETIQUETTE: 101 Ways to Conduct Business with Charm & Savvy- Second Edition*, (Franklin Lakes: The Career Press, Inc., 2002), 94.
[102] Sabath. *BUSINESS ETIQUETTE*, 94.

when I am obsessed with meeting up with a target, don't just come close. Like right now I am determined to publish ten to fifteen books this year. So I hardly give attention to most people, my phone, the internet, and I even eat very little. I do not want to wait until the end of the year when there is no time then I will start reacting. I am using every available time at my disposal now to act rather than react when the time is slim.

When I published Tripartite Battlegrounds and gave a complimentary copy to one of my professors—Cephas Tushima, he looked at the book of almost 400 pages, he knew I was at the time doing my graduate studies and would not have had time to work on a book. In his amazement, he asked. "Where in the world did you get the time to write such a book?" my response was, "I work like a bat." While most people are sleeping that's when I write.

I can not tell everyone to choose nights as their prime time. The nature of what you do, in conjunction with how you have trained your body to cope, will determine your prime time.

Ann further says:

For some people, it is the beginning of the day before phones start ringing and people begin dropping. For others, the end of the workday is "prime time." Maybe you have a different nominee for your own "prime time"—but there is an hour or two of time when you can train yourself to get your best work done. Make the most of it![103]

The whole essence of planning your time is to keep your goals in view. Kiyosaki calls this "keeping the big picture in view". In his very words he says:

One way to maintain control is to always keep the big picture in mind. When people talk about the big picture, I am often reminded of a tapestry. Someone once told me that if you look at the back of a beautiful and priceless tapestry, all you will see is a bunch of knots. Well, sometimes that's all people will see because they haven't seen the finished design on the other side yet. Destiny sometimes works that way, so don't give up control by leaving your own tapestry—the design of your life—unfinished[104]

---

[103] Sabath. *BUSINESS ETIQUETTE,* 94.
[104] Trump and Kiyosaki. *Why we want you to be rich,* 137.

When you manage your time well, it helps you to focus on the big picture—your goals—and gives you the mastery of taking control of situations even when your priceless tapestry is seeming to people as just a bunch of knots. They have not seen the finished design on the other side yet, so what you are doing may not make sense to them.

Keep at it friend. Do not give up control because of the challenges you are going through destiny. Do not leave your very priceless tapestry —the design of your life—unfinished or unattended to as many have done.

f.   Consistency is cause and effects

Nothing just happens, "Everything happens for a reason; for every effect, there is a specific cause." This statement by Tracy is born from Aristotle's law of cause and effect. He stated that "everything happens for a reason, whether or not we know what it is. He said that every effect has a specific cause or causes. Every cause or action has an effect of some kind, whether we can see it and whether we like it or not."[105]

---

[105] Tracy. *The 100 Absolutely unbreakable law of business success,* 14.

Tracy further says that "Achievement, wealth, happiness, prosperity, and business success are all the direct and indirect effects or results of specific causes or actions."[106] Tracy interprets the law to mean that, "if you can be clear about the effect or result you want, you can probably achieve it. You can study others who have achieved the same goal, and by doing what they did, you can get the same result"[107]

This law was not necessarily compounded by man but by God himself. His word says, *"As long as the earth endures, seedtime and harvest, cold and heat, summer and winter, day and night will never cease."[108] Remember this: Whoever sows sparingly will also reap sparingly, and whoever sows generously will also reap generously.[109]*

I will never tell you I am a lucky man. I am a child of destiny who deliberately works hard to achieve my goals. Miracles do happen but success is not one of

---

106 Tracy. *The 100 Absolutely unbreakable law of business success,* 14.
107 Tracy. *The 100 Absolutely unbreakable law of business success,* 14.
108 Genesis 8:22. New International Version.
109 2 Corinthians 9:6. New International Version.

them, neither is luck. Success is the fruit of creativity, commitment, and the consistency which you have sowed in achieving your goals.

When you sow laziness, idleness, inactivity, and nonsense, you will also reap exactly what you have sowed. I do not understand the blame game when a person is lazy and wants to succeed. A hard-working student that gets "A's" will boldly tell you I got an "A", but a lazy student fails and tells you, the lecturer has given me an "F". If as a student, you work hard to achieve your success goals by sowing time to give attention to your lectures and spend extra time reading and researching, your success goals will be achieved.

A business person that wants to succeed will study from the masters in business. A pastor who wants to succeed will learn from the pastors who are succeeding. An artist who wants to succeed will learn from successful artists. The musician who wants to succeed will learn from musicians who have succeeded. A politician who wants to succeed will learn from successful politicians and do the things which made them succeed by avoiding the areas they failed.

You have gone a great length to make sure you succeed. So why will you sow bad seeds that are worthless? Why would you generate good ideas that are capable of making you succeed yet sow laziness in your success project? And why would you give up at this point when you are so close to your consummation—breakthrough? Keep at it, the seed of hard work and dedication pays. Do your part of the planning and watering your success seed, and allow God to do his part. Paul discoursing about the issues of life brought up these words and they also fit this concept of success. He says:

> The one who plants and the one who waters really do not matter. It is God who matters, because he makes the plant grow. There is no difference between the one who plants and the one who waters; God will reward each one according to the work each has done.[110]

The good news here is that you are the one doing the planting and most of the watering on your vision. So just keep at it, your maker who established the law of sowing and reaping will cause the desired increase to your seed. Just be patient, seeds do not grow in a day. And please, do

---

[110] 1 Corinthians 3:7-8. Good News Translation.

not try to jump the process. Growth takes time but success does surely come. Your harvest time is nearer, friend!

7. Success: Its Dangers

The danger of success is that
it makes us forget the world's
dreadful injustice.
-Jules Renard

THE GIVER OF SUCCESS EVEN TO THE ONES that fail to acknowledge his existence, is God. He was the one that actually put down the laws of success engraved then in creation and in the hearts of people. No knowledge is independent of him. Just like a person who uses a source or idea without acknowledging his or her source is called a plagiarist, I should rather say a person who is successful and refuses to acknowledge God as his or her source of success has committed Theogiarism[111].

---

[111] Theogiarism is not in any dictionary I know of. I did not even find it on any search engine on the internet. It is my coined word for people who refuse to acknowledge God—the giver of all success; for making them succeed.

The rich fool

Many people have reached a point of success in their lives that they boast in their achievements as if their planting and watering was all they needed without the creator's increase. Jesus once told a story about such people who commit Theogiarism and said:

> ...The farm of a certain rich man produced a terrific crop. He talked to himself: 'What can I do? My barn isn't big enough for this harvest.' Then he said, 'here's what I'll do: I'll tear down my barns and build bigger ones. Then I'll gather in all my grain and goods, and I'll say to myself, self, you've done well! You've got it made and can now retire. Take it easy and have the time of your life!' "Just then God showed up and said, 'Fool! Tonight you die. And your barnful of goods — who gets it?' "That's what happens when you fill your barn with self and not with God."[112]

This rich man is called "the rich fool" by many people because he failed to acknowledge his maker. The tendency for people to think that it is only hard work that pays is there. This disposition makes

---

[112] Luke 12:16-21. The Message.

them arrogant and proud. I have seen very few successful people with a calm head. I am not just limiting this to money. People who have attained academic success in many cases will want you to know about their certificates and titles. So are politicians, pastors, business people and any endeavour that brings success.

Tread with caution

No person is born a success even if they think they were born with a silver spoon. It takes training and development for you to attain financial and any kind of success. For the reason that you were probably unsuccessful before you climbed to the level of success you have attained, the place of God must be recognized.

Friend, tread with caution. Many people went up the pyramid; but because of mismanagement, they came down to its bottom. When a person is arrogant, the setbacks in life that bring them low can be a major blow that makes it difficult for them to recover.

There is no reason you should come down to the bottom of the pyramid if you hold to these God-given principles outlined in this material. But be careful not to be proud, arrogant, inconsiderate, selfish, and Godless as many successful people have become. Do not become a god in yourself, making the creator your rival.

Do not forget your maker

The rich man we earlier mentioned felt that he is all he needs to be with the help of no one. He just wanted to accumulate and enjoy himself, and the story said, *"Just then God showed up and said, 'Fool! Tonight you die. And your barnful of goods — who gets it?' "That's what happens when you fill your barn with Self and not with God."* Do not let success take the better part of you. Do not forget your maker because you are successful. When you are truly successful:

> ...that is the time to be careful! Beware that in your plenty you do not forget the LORD your God and disobey his commands, regulations, and decrees that I am giving you today. For when you have become full and prosperous and have built fine homes to live in, and when your flocks and herds have become very large and your silver and gold have multiplied along with everything else, be careful! Do not become proud at that time and forget the LORD your

God... He did all this so you would never say to yourself, 'I have achieved this wealth with my own strength and energy.' Remember the LORD your God. He is the one who gives you power to be successful, in order to fulfill the covenant ...[113]

So rather than puff yourself with *SELF* because of your success, fill yourself with God. Success without God is not true success because it does not have eternal value. Such success is a sure way for an eternal disconnect.

---

[113] Deuteronomy 8:11-14, 17, 18. New Living Translation.

8. Success: What for?

You weren't born just to live a life and to die; you were born to accomplish something specific. Matter of fact, success is making it to the end of your purpose; that is success... Success is not just existing. Success is making it to the end of why you were born.
-Myles Munroe

You were born for a reason, which is why with the over 7.8 billion people in the world as at January 2020, your creator made you unique. He wired you with a distinctive purpose but leaves you to decide how you go about accomplishing the purpose in your own style.

He knows you

God affirmed this when spoke to one of his spokespersons saying, *"I knew you before you were formed within your mother's womb; before you were born I sanctified you and appointed you as my spokesman to the world.*"[114] This does not mean that when your maker says he knows you and what you were born to do, then you do not have a part to play about your destiny.

Generally, all people were born to glorify God, for a relationship with him and their fellow human beings, and for service to him, humanity, and for the ecology. We do this by discovering our specific purpose which helps us to accomplish our destinies.

Because we all have our specific missions on this side of life, there is a dire need for us to succeed in our endeavours by getting all available resources be they material, human, or any other resource that can help us accomplish our life goal.

Fitting into his program

A wise person at all times thinks in relation to why he or she was created. I have categorically said in several places in this book that, the purpose of every person on earth is to glorify God, for a healthy relationship with God and all humanity, for service to God, humanity, and for the ecology. This

---

[114] Jeremiah 1:5. The Living Bible.

understanding should stir each one of us to find out how they specifically fit into this God's program by understanding their personal purpose.

With the understanding of purpose, it brings clarity to what success is meant for. Success is meant for fulfilling your purpose on earth. When you know your purpose and you are maximizing your potentials, it should drive you to sow seeds of kindness to the lives of people. Unfortunately, many people hoard their successes for themselves. Many people with financial success keep accumulating until the obsession makes them behave as if the humanity in them is deleted by their own hands. Many financially rich people I know are very stingy to the detriment of their investment in the celestial city. Jesus warns:

> Do not gather and heap up and store up for yourselves treasures on earth, where moth and rust and worm consume and destroy, and where thieves break through and steal. But gather and heap up and store for yourselves treasures in heaven, where neither moth nor rust nor worm consume and destroy, and where thieves do not

break through and steal; for where your treasure is, there will your heart be also.[115]

The celestial bank

The best way to invest in the life beyond is to give out. Riches can develop wings and fly away, but investment in your celestial bank will be forever. Do not think that heaven does not take into account what you do to your wealth. You will be definitely judged by how you spend your income be it in knowledge, your abilities or in financial wealth. Accumulating wealth only for your self is detrimental. Bruce Barton tells about the two seas in Palestine saying:

> One is fresh, and fish are in it. Splashes of green adorn its banks. Trees spread their branches over it and stretch out their thirsty roots to sip of its healing waters.

> The River Jordan makes this sea with sparkling water from the hills. So it laughs in the sunshine. And men build their houses near to it, and birds their nests; and every kind of life is happier because it is there.

---

[115] Mathew 6:19-21. Amplified Version.

The River Jordan flows on out into another sea. Here there is no splash of fish, no fluttering leaf, no song of birds, no children's laughter. Travelers choose another route, unless on urgent business. The air hangs heavy above its water, and neither man nor beast nor fowl will drink.

What makes this mighty difference in these neighbor seas? Note, the River Jordan. It empties the same good water into both. Not the soil in which they lie; not in the country round about.

This is the difference.

The Sea of Galilee receives but does not keep the Jordan. For every drop that flows into it, another drop flows out. The giving and receiving go on in equal measure. The other sea is shrewder, hoarding its income jealously. It will not be tempted into any generous impulse. Every drop it gets, it keeps.

The Sea of Galilee gives and lives. This other sea gives nothing. It is named Dead.

There are two kinds of people in this world. They are two seas in Palestine. [116]

Our life is a conduit pipe. The stuff that comes to us is supposed to get through us to other lives. When we begin to accumulate, our life's become like the Dead Sea which has no fish or any kind of swimming, squirming creatures living in or near the water. Any fish that accidentally enters the Dead Sea from the freshwater streams dies instantly because of the density of salt in it. Do not be the sea of death but be the life-giving sea. Thank you!

---

[116]Bruce Barton. "Two seas in Palestine," [cited August 26, 2015] Online: http://dynamiccatholic.com/give/two-seas-in-palestine/

9. Conclusion

The road to success has to have
obstacles because, at the end of
the day, when success comes, it
will be that much better.
-Shelly-Ann Fraser-Pryce

LIFE IS A GIFT; IT IS A PRIVILEGE THAT IS not enjoyed by all. Your life is a gift to this generation, and you must not leave without scoring your mark. You must not look down on your abilities even if they seem not to be what you so desire. You must look at success in its uniqueness. What is success to me may not be success to you. Your definition of success should be how God defines it. Imagine who God says was successful.

Success is not necessarily money

In ancient Egypt lived a man that was the king's official in charge of the palace guards. This man's wife was interested in having a sexual relationship with their house manager but the manager was a pious young man and ran out of the house in rejection of his boss' wife offer. Out of rage and disappointment, the lady reported the house manager to the husband for sexual harassment and the house manager was thrown into prison "where the king's prisoners were kept. While Joseph [the house manager][117] was in prison, the LORD helped him and was good to him. He even made the jailer like Joseph so much that he put him in charge of the other prisoners and of everything that was done in the jail. The jailer did not worry about anything, because the LORD was with Joseph and made him *successful* in all that he did.[118]

Did I just hear that a prisoner was successful? Yes, he was. Success is not defined by financial success alone but by purpose. When you discover your purpose, maximizing your potentials, and you are sowing gifts of kindness in the lives of people, even if you do not have a financial breakthrough yet, you are successful.

---

[117] The part of the story in italics is from a life manual scrip. (Bible) The house manager in the bracket is added by the author. It's not found in the original scrip.
[118] Genesis 39:19-23. Contemporary English Version.

Gods elevation

Joseph was an interpreter of dreams and he made sure he used his potential maximally. He was also aware of his service and administrative qualities, so in his boss's house, he was the house manager. In prison, he was the manager of other prisoners. And once he was faithful in those little areas, God elevated him—Joseph because he put his potential to use. He later became the governor of all Egypt.

This is what happened on the day of his appointment. The king said:

> I now appoint you governor over all Egypt." The king removed from his finger the ring engraved with the royal seal and put it on Joseph's finger. He put a fine linen robe on him, and placed a gold chain around his neck. He gave him the second royal chariot to ride in, and his guard of honor went ahead of him and cried out, "Make way! Make way!" And so Joseph was appointed governor over all Egypt. The king said to him, "I am the king — and no one in all Egypt shall so

much as lift a hand or a foot without your permission."[119]

Joseph's success did not start when he became the governor of Egypt. It started when he discovered his purpose and began to maximize his potential as a dreamer and administrator. When he started using his abilities to be a blessing to people based on his purpose, his prosperity began.

Commit yourself to your creative ideas

Remember, God wants you to be successful and he has put his creative abilities in you. Your part in the success journey is to discover your purpose for living and start maximizing your potentials. This will lead you to do creative things that will help you to accomplish your success goals. Commit yourself to your creative ideas, and be consistent with making sure that those God-given ideas come to fruition.

Do not underestimate yourself. You are more powerful than you can imagine. You have the breath of God in you, and what that means is that

---

[119] Genesis 41:41-44. Good News Translation

there is nothing you cannot do, once you put your heart to it. Nelson Mandela a vile man like you and I understood our innermost abilities and reiterated Marianne Williamson saying:

> Our deepest fear is not that we are inadequate. Our deepest fear is that we are powerful beyond measure. It is our light, not our darkness that most frightens us. We ask ourselves, who am I to be brilliant, gorgeous, talented, fabulous? Actually, who are you not to be?"[120]

Yes, who are you not to be, when God has put in you all you need to be who you were born to be? You do not have a choice not to succeed. All you need to succeed is within you. *"Remember the LORD your God. He is the one who gives you power to be successful, in order to fulfil the covenant..."*[121] All the energy you need is within. You are brilliant, gorgeous, talented, fabulous and wired for success. More so, your maker brings destiny helpers your way

---

[120] Julie. *ACHIEVING YOUR POTENTIAL: The Higher the Mountain, The Better the View when you arrive,* (julie@ariadnecapital.com, 2006), 15.
[121] Deuteronomy 8:18. New Living Translation

to water your endeavours. Child of destiny! Rise up, it is your time to succeed! Yes, it is

Bibliography

Allen, James. *As a man thinketh.* (St. Augustine: AsAManThinketh.net, 2001)

Bastian, Bob. *404 improvement tips.* (Sumatera Selatan: Bob Bastian and omniwebmarketing.com, 2004)

Burton, Kate and Platts, Brinley. *Building Confidence for Dummies.* (West Sussex: John Wiley & Sons, Ltd, 2006)

Evolution Team and Evolution readers. *22 Powerful Tools to Transform Your Fear into Happiness, Peace and Inspiration.* (www.FreeFromFear.com and www.EvolutionEzine.com, 2009)

Julie. *ACHIEVING YOUR POTENTIAL: The Higher the Mountain, The Better the View when you arrive.* (julie@ariadnecapital.com, 2006)

Lee, Michael. *21 Powerful Ways to Persuade People to Do What You Want.* (www.20daypersuasion.com)

Maxwell, John C. *Your road map for success.* (Nashville: Thomas Nelson, Inc., 2002)

Munroe, Myles. *The spirit of leadership: cultivating the attitudes that influence human action.* (New Kensington: Whitaker house, 2005)

__________ *Maximizing your potentials.* (Nassau: Destiny image publishing, 2002)

__________ *Understanding your potentials.* (Nassau: Destiny image publishing, 2002)

Musa, Danladi. *The strategic Planning Process.* (Jos: CAPRO Media,1999)

Nikitina, Arina. *The five laws of success.* (United Kingdom: White Dove Books, 2006)

Preston, David Lawrence. *360 steps to Self-confidence.* (Oxford: How to book LTD, 2001)

Robbins, Anthony. *Awaken the giant within.* (New York: Free Press, 1991)

Sabath, Ann Marie. *BUSINESS ETIQUETTE: 101 Ways to Conduct Business with Charm & Savvy- Second Edition.* (Franklin Lakes: The Career Press, Inc., 2002)

Slater, Robert. *29 Leadership Secrets from Jack Welch.* (New York: The McGraw-Hill Companies, Inc., 2003)

Swinton, Lyndsay. *Goal Setting Guide.* (United Kingdom: Uncommon Knowledge Ltd, 2006)

Tracy, Brian. *The 100 absolutely Unbreakable laws of business success.* (San Francisco: Berrett-Koehler Publishers, Inc., 2000)

Trump, Donald. *TRUMP How to Get Rich.* (New York: Random House, 2004)

Trump, Donald J. and Kiyosaki, Robert T. *Why we want you to be rich.* (New York: Rich Press, 2006)

Waugh, Troy. *101 Marketing Strategies for Accounting, Law, Consulting, and Professional Services Firms.* (Hoboken, New Jersey: John Wiley & Sons, Inc., 2004)

Internet Resources

Barton, Bruce. "Two seas in Palestine." Cited 26 August 2015. Online: http://dynamiccatholic.com/give/two-seas-in-palestine/

Boulder Coaching Academy. "Affirmation." Cited 21 August 2015. Online: http://www.bouldercoachingacademy.com/affirmations/what-is-an-affirmation-they-will-change-your-life-forever/

Business Dictionary. "Definition of Success." Cited 18 August 2015. Online: www.businessdictionary.com/definition/success.html

California State University Northridge. "Definition of Creativity." Cited 19 August 2015. Online: http://www.csun.edu/~vcpsy00h/creativity/define.htm.

Cambridge Dictionary. Definition of commitment." Cited 18 August 2015. Online: http://dictionary.cambridge.org/dictionary/english/commitment.

Evolution Team and Evolution Readers. "22 Powerful Tools to Transform Your Fear into Happiness, Peace and Inspiration." Cited 18 August 2015. Online: www.FreeFromFear.com and www.EvolutionEzine.com

Forlearn. "Foresight." Cited 18 August 2015. Online: http://forlearn.jrc.ec.europa.eu/guide/1_why-foresight/characteristics.htm.

Innovation management. "How do you define innovation and make it practical and saleable to senior management." Cited 18 August 2015. Online: http://www.innovationmanagement.se/imtool-articles/how-do-you-define-innovation-

and-make-it-practical-and-saleable-to-senior-management/

Kurtu, Ron. "Failures of Abraham Lincoln (1800s)." Cited 18 August 2015. Online: http://www.school-for-champions.com/history/lincoln_failures

Mindtools, "NewTMC." Cited 18 August 2015. Online: http://www.mindtools.com/pages/article/newTMC_05.htm.

Motivation for Dreamers. "What is Success." Cited 18 August 2015. Online: www.motivation-for-dreamers.com/whatissuccess.html.

Oxford Dictionary. "Definition of Desire." Cited 18 August 2015. Online: www.oxforddictionaries.com/definition/english/desire.

__________. "Definition of clarity." Cited 18 August 2015. Online: www.oxforddictionaries.com/definition/english/clarity.

__________. "Definition of belief." Cited 18 August 2015. Online: www.oxforddictionaries.com/definition/engl ish/

Pavey, Sarah and the Mind Tools Team, "Eisenhower's Urgent/Important Principle." Cited 21 August 2015. Online: http://www.mindtools.com/pages/article/ne wHTE_91.htm.

Success Consciousness. "Affirmation." Cited 21 August 2015. Online: http://www.successconsciousness.com/affir mations.htm.

Wikipedia, "The life of Nick Vujicic," Cited 18 August 2015. Online: http://en.wikipedia.org/wiki/Nick_Vujicic

Other resources

Giberston, Jim. *PC Study Bible V5.oC*. (Seattle: Biblesoft. www. Biblesoft.com, 2006)

Merriam-Webster dictionary. Android application 2015.

Meyers, Rick. *E-sword Bible Version 10.4.0.* (Franklin USA: www.e-sword. net, 2014)

Other Books from Scrollhouse

Book for a Seminar

Scrollhouse Publishing Firm (A service of TheTheShepherd Loho-u-Ter Resources) conducts the following seminars and workshops:

-Authoring Masterclass
-Junior Authoring Masterclass
-Life Coaching workshop
-Editing workshop
-Leadership Workshops
-Admin Seminar
-Success Workshops
-Marriage Seminars

Contact us and book for a seminar in your organization.

scrollhouseng@gmail.com
www.scrollhouse.com.ng
+234-805-346-8634
+234-803-208-8168